"In the Inspector Morse books and screenplays, the physical presence of Oxford has been of great significance, and the paintings in this book admirably reflect the City's magnificent and varied architecture. It is a great compliment to Oxford that such distinguished members of the Royal Watercolour Society have produced these evocative views."

Colin Dexter, OBE
Oxford

For my mother and father, IRENE and CHARLES

First published in Great Britain in 2001 by

CONTEMPORARY WATERCOLOURS LIMITED
165 Parrock Street,
Gravesend
Kent DA12 1ER

Tel: 01474 535922

Website: www.contemwatercolours.fsnet.co.uk

Designers and editorial consultants: Bass Walker Associates, Sevenoaks

Set in Garamond. Artwork by Janet Davie. Project co-ordinator: Susan Grant

Printed by Grafiche Milani, S.pA., Italy. Scans by Morgan Baker, Ashford, Kent

ISBN 09526480 1 6

Front cover: ***Hertford – Bridge of Sighs*** *(Dennis Flanders)*
Back Cover: ***Queens – View from the High*** *(John Doyle);* ***Hertford – OB Quad*** *(Dennis Flanders);*
Lincoln – Turl Street *(Jane Carpanini);* ***Oriel – Front Quadrangle*** *(Ken Howard);* ***Pembroke – Pembroke Square*** *(Dennis Roxby Bott)*

OXFORD WATERCOLOURS

Views of the university and colleges by members of the Royal Watercolour Society

**Jane Carpanini John Doyle Dennis Flanders
Ken Howard Dennis Roxby Bott**

Text by
MALCOLM HORTON

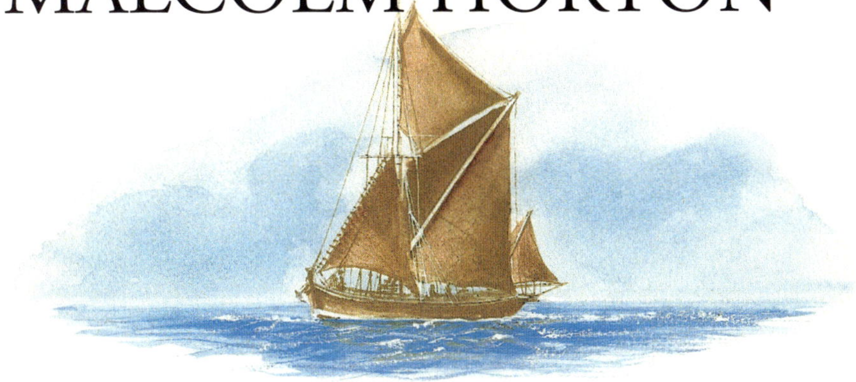

CONTEMPORARY WATERCOLOURS

The Royal Watercolour Society

The Royal Watercolour Society was founded in 1804 and received its Royal Patronage in 1884. It is the oldest society of its kind in the world. Society members have included Peter De Wint, David Cox, Helen Allingham, John Sell Cotman, Samuel Palmer, Sir Edward Burne Jones, John Singer Sargent, Arthur Rackham, Sir William Russell Flint and Charles Knight.

The Society is now based at the Bankside Gallery, which is situated on the South Bank of the River Thames overlooking St Paul's Cathedral. The gallery was opened on 11th November, 1980 by Her Majesty the Queen. The area is of great historical importance and, with the opening of the new Tate Gallery of Modern Art, is now the focus for the best contemporary art. There are some 90 Members of the Royal Watercolour Society, both Fellows and Associates, and admission to the Society is determined by annual election.

Jane Carpanini *RWS, RBA, RWA*

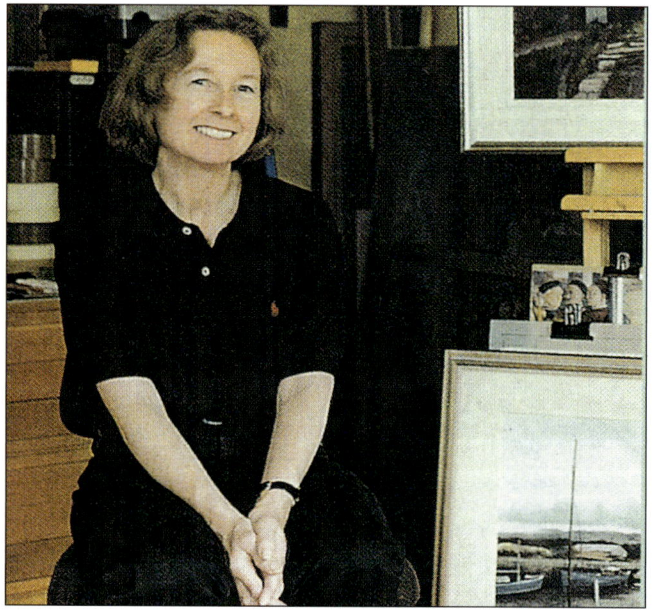

Jane was born in Bedfordshire in 1949. She was elected to the Royal Watercolour Society in 1978, establishing a reputation for expansively composed and meticulous watercolours. She was trained at Brighton College of Art and the University of Reading.

Her work is in the collections of the National Library and the National Museum of Wales. She is also a member of the Royal West of England Academy and of the Royal Society of British Artists, and exhibits regularly within these societies.

Jane has served as the Vice-President and is currently Honorary Treasurer of the Royal Watercolour Society.

In 1983 she was the winner of the prestigious Hunting Groups Prize for the Watercolour of the Year by a British Artist.

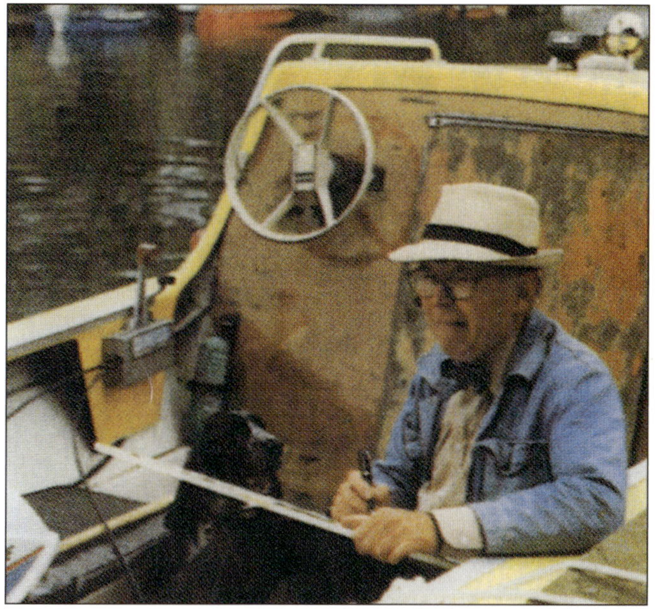

John Doyle *MBE, PPRWS*

Born in Dulwich, London, in 1928, John is immediate past-President of the Royal Watercolour Society. He has had many exhibitions in major galleries in London and in Canterbury Cathedral. His book, entitled An Artist's Journey Down the Thames, *was published in 1989.*

He has recently undertaken a peripatetic journey retracing, and painting in, St Augustine's footsteps from Rome to Canterbury to celebrate, in 1997, the fourteenth centenary of that famous event. This culminated in an exhibition at Canterbury Cathedral of the 300 or so paintings made during the course of John's journey.

John now lives on the edge of Romney Marsh in Kent, and readily acknowledges the help and encouragement he received in the early years from the distinguished painter John Ward.

Dennis Flanders *RWS, RBA*

Born in London in 1915, Dennis was unquestionably one of the greatest pencil and watercolour artists of the twentieth century. He attended evening classes in antique drawing at the Regent Street Polytechnic while working for a firm of fashionable interior decorators. He painted the scenery and architecture of the British Isles for more than sixty years before his death in 1994.

Dennis has been described as the "Canaletto of our time" by Peterborough in The Daily Telegraph *and was, for some years, a graphic reporter with the* Illustrated London News. *His pictures of London during the Blitz are treasures of the Guildhall Library and the Imperial War Museum.*

A Freeman of the City of London, he was a member of the Art Workers Guild and served as Master in 1975. Two previous books have been published containing the body of his lifetime's work: Britannia *in 1984, and* Watercolours in Academe *in 1995.*

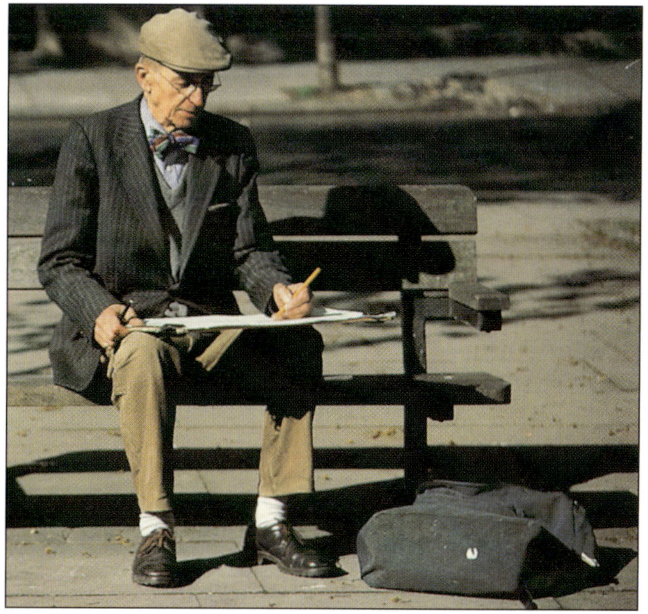

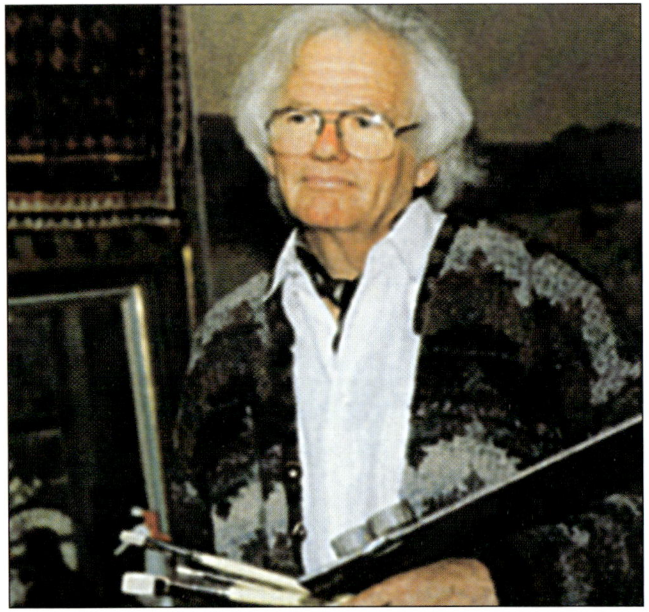

Ken Howard RA, RWS

Ken was born in London in 1932, and is a member of the Royal Academy and of the Royal Watercolour Society. He is also President of the New English Arts Club, that bastion of figurative painting and drawing, and was official war artist in Northern Ireland in 1973 and 1978.

Since his National Service in the Royal Marines, 1953-1955, he has had a close association with the British Army undertaking special commissions for them throughout the world, including portraits of the Royal Family. Ken's work is held in public collections including the Imperial War Museum, Ulster Museum, National Army Museum and the Guildhall Art Gallery.

He has studios in London and Cornwall, and two books on his life and works have been published: The Paintings of Ken Howard *in 1992, and* Ken Howard, a Personal View *in 1998.*

Dennis Roxby Bott RWS

Born in Chingford, Essex, in 1948, Dennis attended the prestigious Norwich School of Art where he studied fine art painting and obtained a Dip.AD (Fine Art). He was elected to the Royal Watercolour Society in 1981.

Dennis, who now lives in Sussex, has had regular one-man exhibitions in London and Sussex, notably Ebury Street Galleries, London, SW1, Worthing Art Gallery and Museum, Lannards Gallery Billingshurst, and the Ogle Galleries.

He is a regular exhibitor at the annual spring and autumn Royal Watercolour Society exhibitions at the Bankside Gallery, and in 1992 he was a prizewinner at the annual Discerning Eye Exhibition at The Mall Gallery in London. His commissions include The Wardroom of HM Royal Yacht Britannia, *and work for Sotheby's, American Express, and the National Trust.*

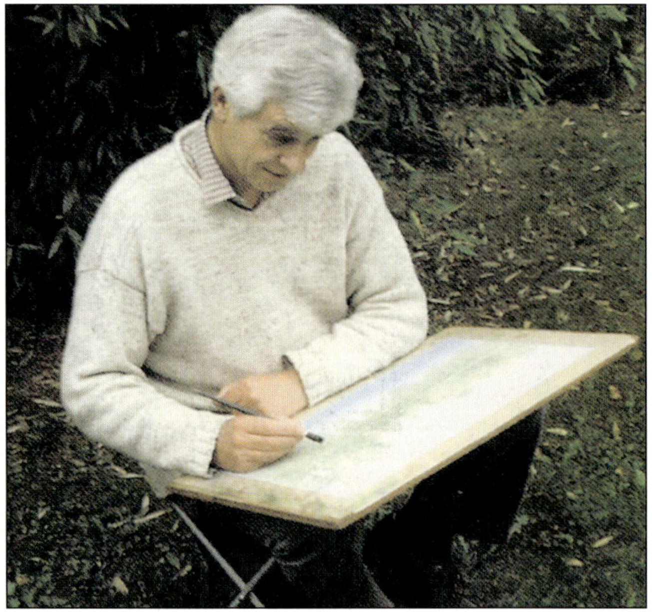

CONTENTS

FOREWORD

By the President of the Royal Watercolour Society

The watercolour art form has, since the mid-18th century, become a quintessentially British genre associated with the unique beauty of the native landscape. In its topographical form with its prerequisite precise drawing, it blends fine architecture with its complimentary landscape. This can clearly be seen in Turner's early work, particularly his many watercolours of Oxford.

This high period of British watercolour painting was the hundred or so years after the mid-18th century. The work of Turner, Constable, De Wint, Palmer, Girtin, Cotman and Sandby popularized the watercolour art form, and led in 1804 to the foundation of the Royal Watercolour Society, the oldest organization of its kind in the world.

Today this great tradition is carried on by the present 90 members, and none more so than the five contributors to this book of Oxford watercolours. I have known all of these distinguished members of the Royal Watercolour Society for many years and it gives me great pleasure to see their work being disseminated to the widest possible audience through the publication of this unique book.

Oxford has always held a fascination for the topographical artist – from the 17th century draughtsman David Loggan, to Buckler and Turner in the 19th century, and the 20th century Hanslip Fletcher and Muirhead Bone. It is fitting, therefore, that we should commence the 21st century with some of our most recent exponents of topographical watercolour using Oxford as the basis for this wonderful collection of paintings.

Francis Bowyer, PRWS
Chiswick, London

INTRODUCTION

Although the watercolours reproduced in this book are associated with particular colleges, they are inextricably linked to Oxford the City and, of course, Oxford the University.

Oxford University is an association which comprises thirty-nine colleges and numerous libraries, laboratories and museums. It crucially administers the lectures and examinations. The Hebdomadal Council is the executive body which runs the University and has representatives from the Colleges.

All students are members of a college which hosts them during their time in Oxford. The college selects them and, thereafter, accommodates them, feeds them and supervises their studies.

The genesis for this collection of watercolours is the series of limited edition prints of Oxford colleges which my company, Contemporary Watercolours, has produced over the past twelve years under the generic title *Contemporary Oxford.* Most have started life as joint projects with the colleges featured, and all have appeared regularly in the University magazine *Oxford Today.*

At the outset it was decided that quality and the pursuit of excellence were to be our watchwords. The watercolour medium was selected because it best suits the topographical nature of the subject matter – fine drawing being a prerequisite. To demonstrate our intentions to the world at large, it was decided that we should commission only artists who were members of the Royal Watercolour Society.

It is hard to believe that in twelve years we have produced sixty-seven watercolours of Oxford, forty of which are reproduced in this book. I have been privileged to work with some of the most talented artists in the land and have received unfailing support and hospitality from the Fellows and Heads of House of the colleges represented in this book. I would like to thank all concerned.

Malcolm Horton

Ashford, Kent

ALL SOULS COLLEGE

John Doyle

The Radcliffe Camera from the Great Quad

All Souls was founded in 1438 by Archbishop Chichele to commemorate the dead of the Hundred Years War with France. It is unique in Oxford having neither undergraduate nor graduate pupils, only Fellows and post graduate research workers.

The Front Quadrangle, occupying a fine site on the corner of Catte Street and the High Street, was completed by the end of the 15th century.

The Great Quadrangle was designed by Nicholas Hawksmoor and constructed between 1716 and 1734 to the north of the existing Front Quadrangle, which was perceived as being somewhat cramped. It contains the Codrington Library, the hall and, of course, the famous towers.

John Doyle's painting, however, largely ignores these architectural gems, preferring to use the Great Quadrangle as a vantage point to view one of Oxford's masterpieces, James Gibbs's Radcliffe Camera.

In his will, John Radcliffe left £40,000 for the building of a science library. Following his death in 1714 it took more than 20 years of negotiations to clear the site and then select an architect. Nicholas Hawksmoor suggested the rotunda form, but James Gibbs was the architect eventually chosen to carry out the work.

The Camera is thought to be the first round library in Britain. It was completed in 1748 and features plasterwork in the domed upper room which is quite breathtaking. Thomas Roberts, an Oxford plasterer, was a contributor, having been responsible for the outstanding stucco work at Christ Church, St John's, and Queen's Library.

The Radcliffe Camera is now part of the Bodleian Library, to which it is connected by an underground passage and conveyor belt.

John Doyle felt that undertaking a painting of Gibbs's masterpiece was very daunting, particularly as getting the ellipses right was quite a problem.

He seems, however, to have brought it off beautifully.

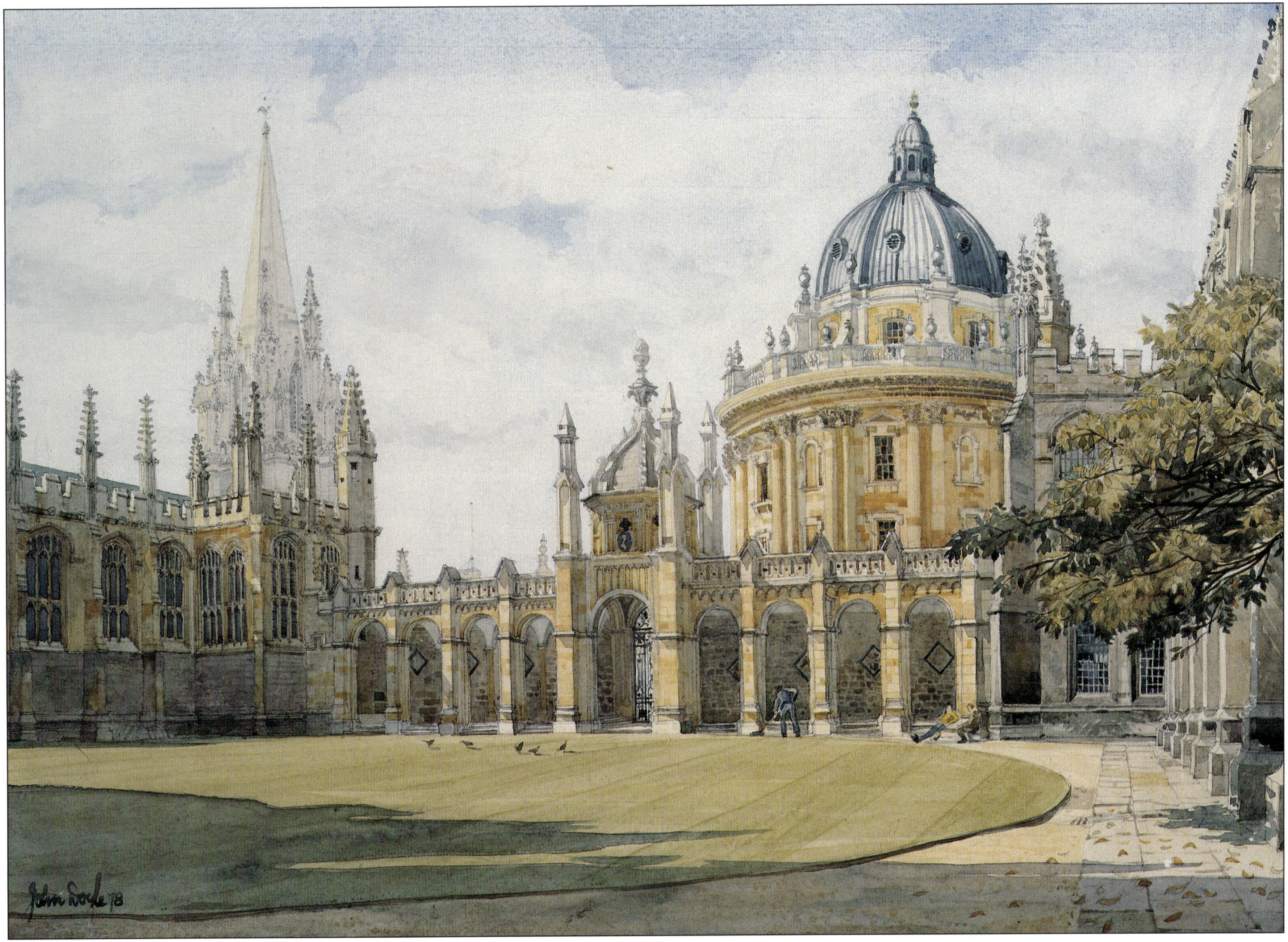
John Doyle 78

BALLIOL COLLEGE

John Doyle

The Garden Quad

Around the year 1255, John de Balliol, Lord of Barnard Castle, grew impatient with the Bishop of Durham over a land dispute and insulted him. As a result John de Balliol was required to do penance, part of which was to provide accommodation in Oxford for impecunious scholars. This consisted of a house standing roughly where the present Master's Lodgings are situated in Broad Street.

Balliol's foundation is officially 1263, thus making it the second oldest college. John de Balliol died in 1269 and it was left to his widow, Dervorguilla of Galloway, to continue and extend her husband's foundation.

It was during the 19th century that the college gained its reputation for academic excellence at the instigation of John Parsons, who was Master from 1798-1819. This pursuit of excellence was continued by successive Masters, including Richard Jenkyns and the charismatic Benjamin Jowett (*"never regret, never explain, never apologize"*).

From the middle of the 19th century, Balliol was virtually rebuilt by a succession of eminent Victorian architects, Waterhouse, Butterfield, Keene and Salvin.

In the centre foreground of John Doyle's painting is Anthony Salvin's Tower (1852). To the right in the background is the Master's Lodgings (1867), designed by Alfred Waterhouse. Its famous oriel window is just discernible.

Probably the most controversial building of this period was William Butterfield's chapel (1853), and his design with its red brick stripes has been much criticized. It can just be seen to the far left in John's painting, and it is clearly a prototype for Butterfield's more homogeneous design for Keble twenty years later.

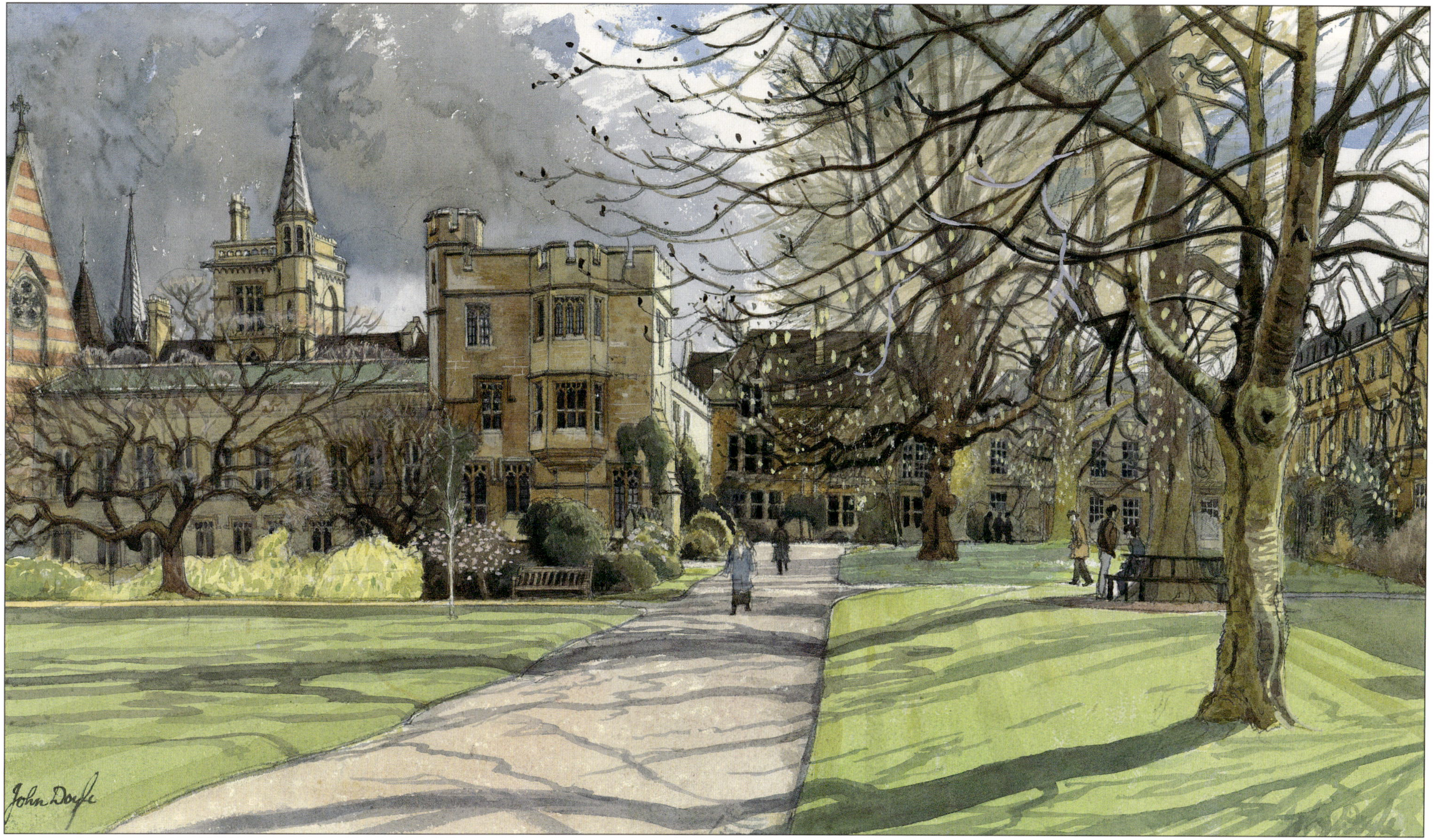
John Doyle

BRASENOSE COLLEGE

Dennis Roxby Bott

The Front Quad

The view through the arch of the Gatehouse is one of Dennis's favourite devices for framing college quads. This one frames beautifully the Front Quadrangle of Brasenose, which dates from 1509, the year of the College's foundation. It is considered to be a fine example of early Tudor domestic architecture, except for the dormer windows which were added in the 17th century to provide extra accommodation in the attic.

The college was founded on the site of several mediaeval halls, the most notable being Brasenose Hall from which the college acquired not only its name but eventually the famous bronze sanctuary knocker or *brazen nose*. The original knocker was taken to Stamford in 1334 by the master and scholars who were themselves seeking sanctuary from the continual rioting between town and gown which characterized Oxford in the 13th and 14th centuries.

Edward II did not approve of this migration and forced the scholars back to Oxford but they did not bring the bronze knocker back with them. It remained on Stamford House until 1890, when the college bought the house to regain possession of the original knocker.

The new college had produced a replica of the knocker at the time of its foundation in 1509 and this is to be found today on the main gate. The original *brazen nose* knocker has pride of place in the Hall hanging over High Table.

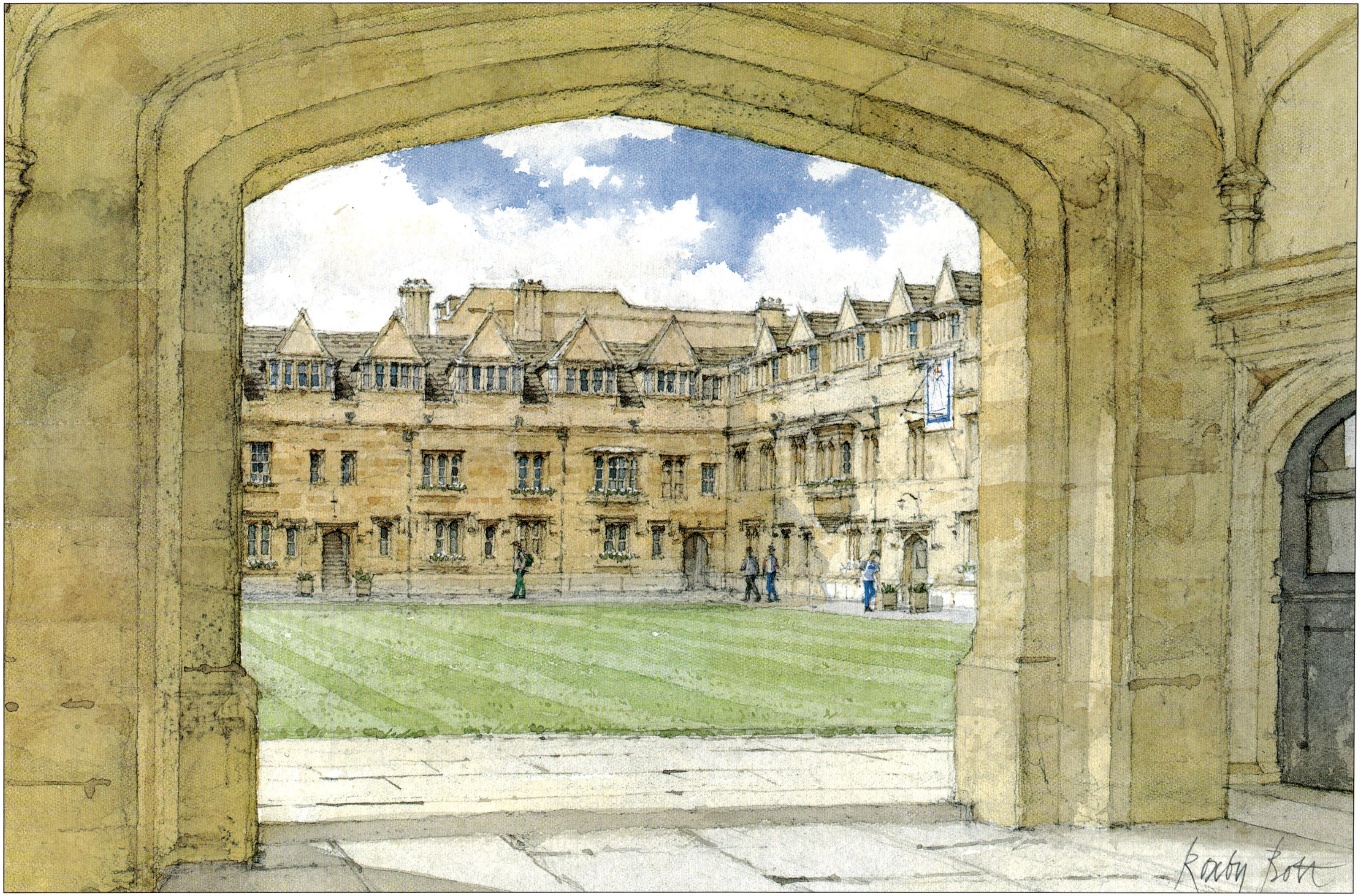

BRASENOSE COLLEGE

Dennis Roxby Bott

View across Radcliffe Square

In Dennis Roxby Bott's painting of the view across the cobbled Radcliffe Square, the gate-tower entrance can be seen on the right and the 17th century chapel on the left.

Although completed in 1666, the oldest part of the chapel is the hammer-beam roof dating from 1440. This was removed from an Augustine Chapel which stood nearby on the site of Frewin Hall and which Brasenose owned.

Views of the front of Brasenose are often drawn from the Bodleian Library looking southwards. Dennis, however, wanted to produce a view with his back to All Souls looking to the west. This achieved a panoramic view of the front of the college with a clear view of the chapel. The Radcliffe Camera normally dominates the Square, but including a small part of it in the foreground of the composition gives depth to the view.

In Colin Dexter's Inspector Morse novels, the fictional Lonsdale College is frequently featured. From the author's precise geographical references Brasenose is obviously the model. This is quite a coincidence because the real-life Bursar of Brasenose, Dr Philip Gasser, was the locations advisor for the Carlton Television series of thirty-three Morse television films. Like the author, Dr Gasser appears in each episode.

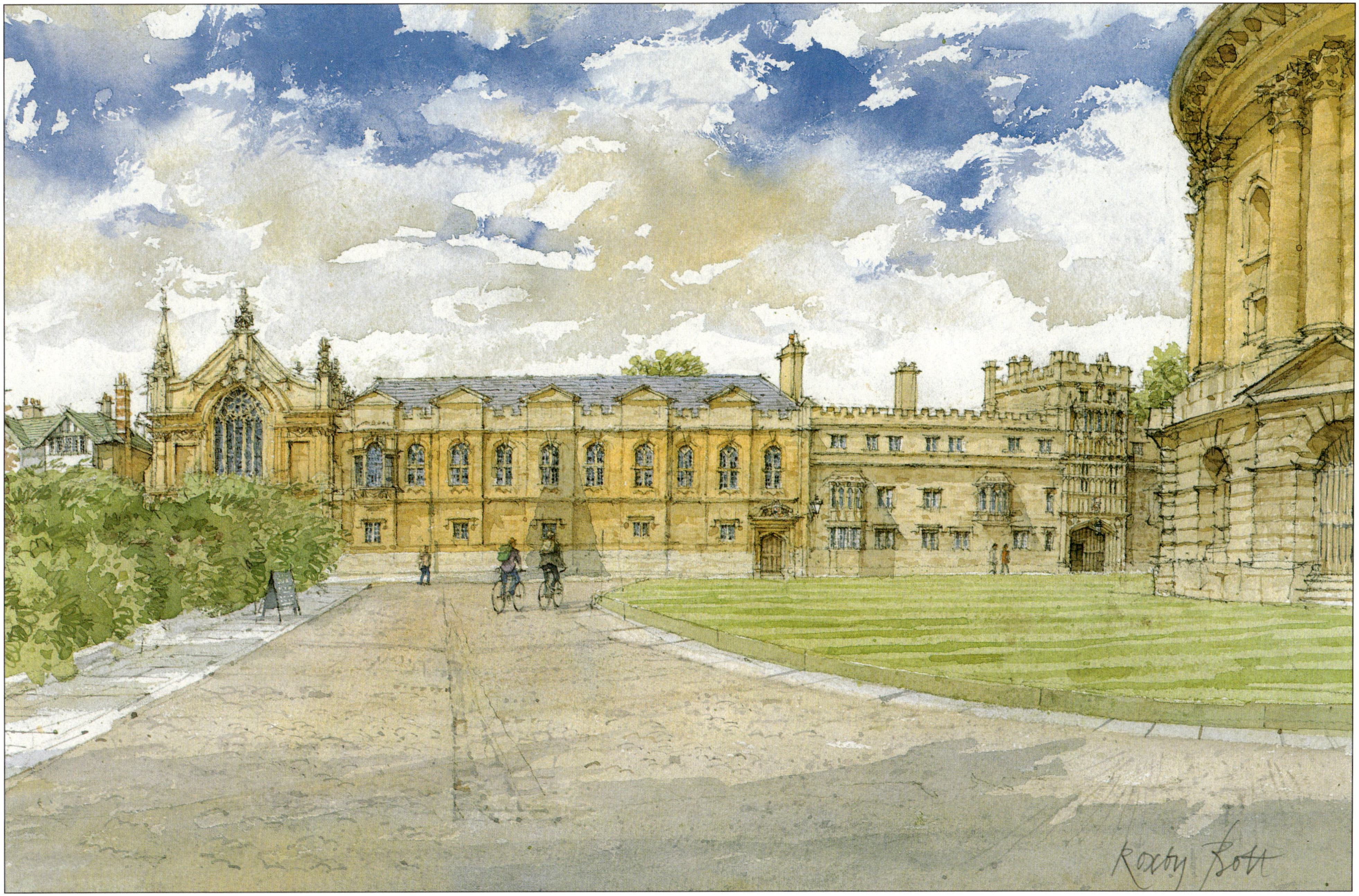
Roxby Bott

CHRIST CHURCH

John Doyle

Tom Tower

Tom Tower is Christ Church's crowning glory, built by Christopher Wren in 1682. It completed Cardinal Thomas Wolsey's western range of building for his original foundation, Cardinal College, which he began in 1525. He was Chancellor to Henry VIII and, next to his monarch, the most powerful man in the land.

Wolsey asset-stripped twenty-two monasteries to provide funds for his new college, which was to be the grandest in all Oxford. Perhaps because it was Oxford's 13th foundation it was inevitable that he should fall from grace, having incurred Henry VIII's displeasure for his extravagant use of power. Henry sacked Wolsey in 1529 and took over and finished the new college, renaming it Christ Church in 1546.

Henry VIII suppressed the nearby Osney Abbey and transferred its bell, originally christened Mary, to Christ Church in 1545. It was re-christened Tom in 1612 after Cardinal Thomas Wolsey.

Re-cast in 1680, it weighs more than seven tons and measures more than seven feet in diameter. Because of its enormous size, it became known as Great Tom. It was installed in Wren's newly completed ogee-capped tower in 1682.

Forty years earlier during the Civil War, (1642 to 1646) Oxford was the Royalist Headquarters and Christ Church was Charles I's royal palace where he held court until his surrender in 1646.

As well as producing thirteen British Prime Ministers, the last being Anthony Eden, Christ Church also had a mathematics don, the Reverend Charles Dodgson, alias Lewis Carroll, the author of *Alice in Wonderland.*

Alice was the real-life daughter of the Dean of Christ Church, Henry Liddel, who held this post from 1855-1891. The post of Dean at Christ Church, unusually, combines ecclesiastical duties with being Head of House of the College.

John Doyle was keen to produce a painting of the impressive street front of Christ Church, and to show Wren's Tom Tower bathed in sunlight so that it would seem to glow like a beacon.

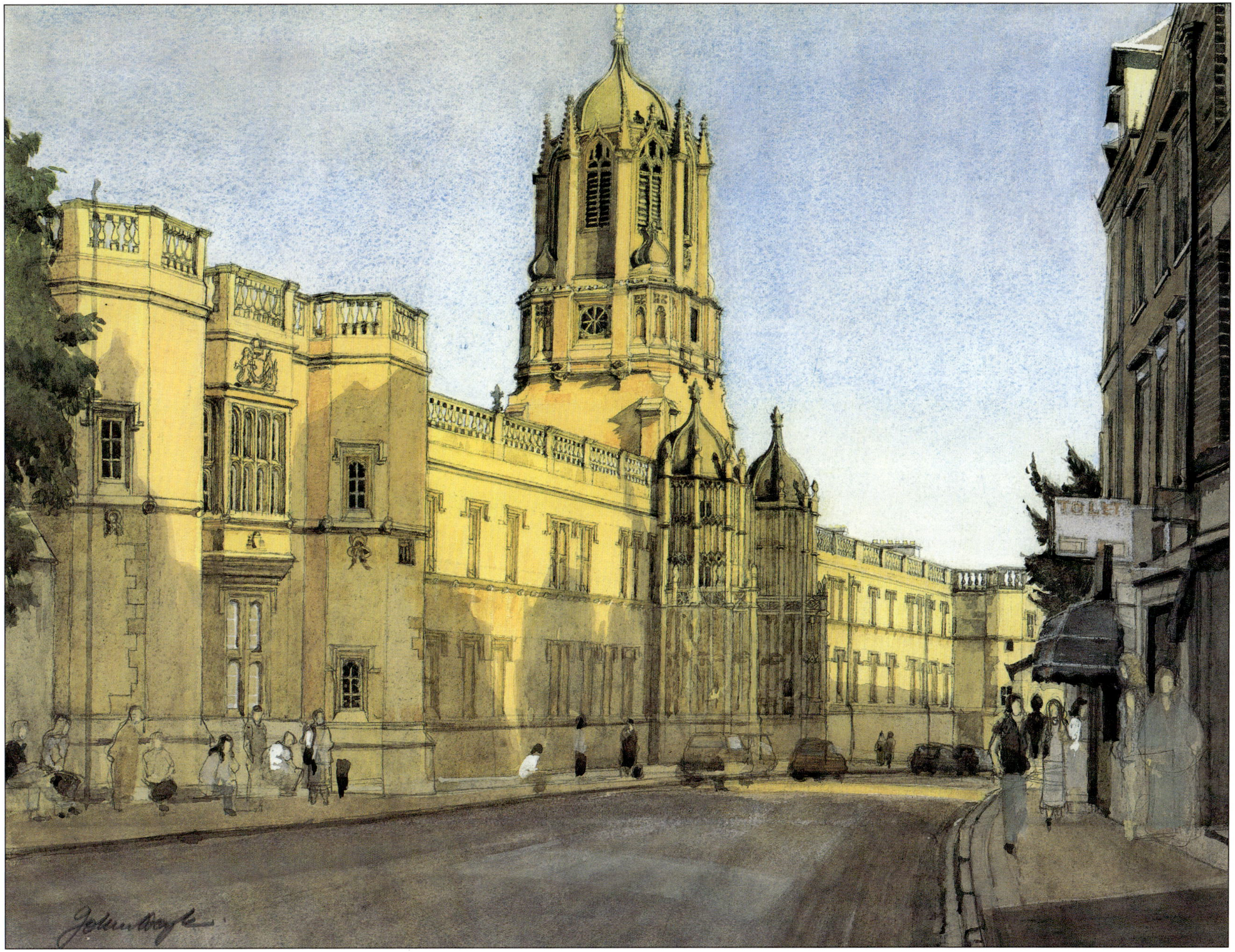
TO LET

CHRIST CHURCH CATHEDRAL

Dennis Flanders

The Chancel Roof

In 1546 Henry VIII designated the former priory church of St Frideswide as Christ Church Cathedral, replacing his 1542 designation, Osney Abbey.

Oxford had until this time been part of the Lincoln diocese. It was on Henry's part an act of rationalization of which any modern day entrepreneur would be proud. He not only effectively closed Osney Abbey and removed its treasures, he also made Christ Church Cathedral the chapel of his new college of Christ Church, although Cardinal Wolsey must take credit for starting the enterprise. In another act of rationalization Henry combined the endowments of church and college, and made the Dean of the Cathedral also head of the new college.

In creating room for his new college Wolsey demolished three bays of St Frideswide's Priory, and it is for this reason that Christ Church is the smallest cathedral in England, although it now has the largest diocese. Another notable feature of Christ Church Cathedral, from its priory days, is its spire, which dates from 1230 and was the first in England. Also of note is the mediaeval glass in the east window of the small chapel of St Lucy, dating from 1320, which depicts the martyrdom of St Thomas a Becket.

For Dennis Flanders the true glory of Christ Church Cathedral was its chancel roof, dating from 1503. With its pendants and intricate vaulting, it was something Dennis had always wanted to draw. He said it was quite the most difficult drawing he had made because of the roof's complicated construction.

Also prominent in the painting is the rose window and the two round-headed windows beneath, completed during Sir George Gilbert Scott's extensive restoration in 1870-1876 and executed by stained-glass makers, Clayton and Bell.

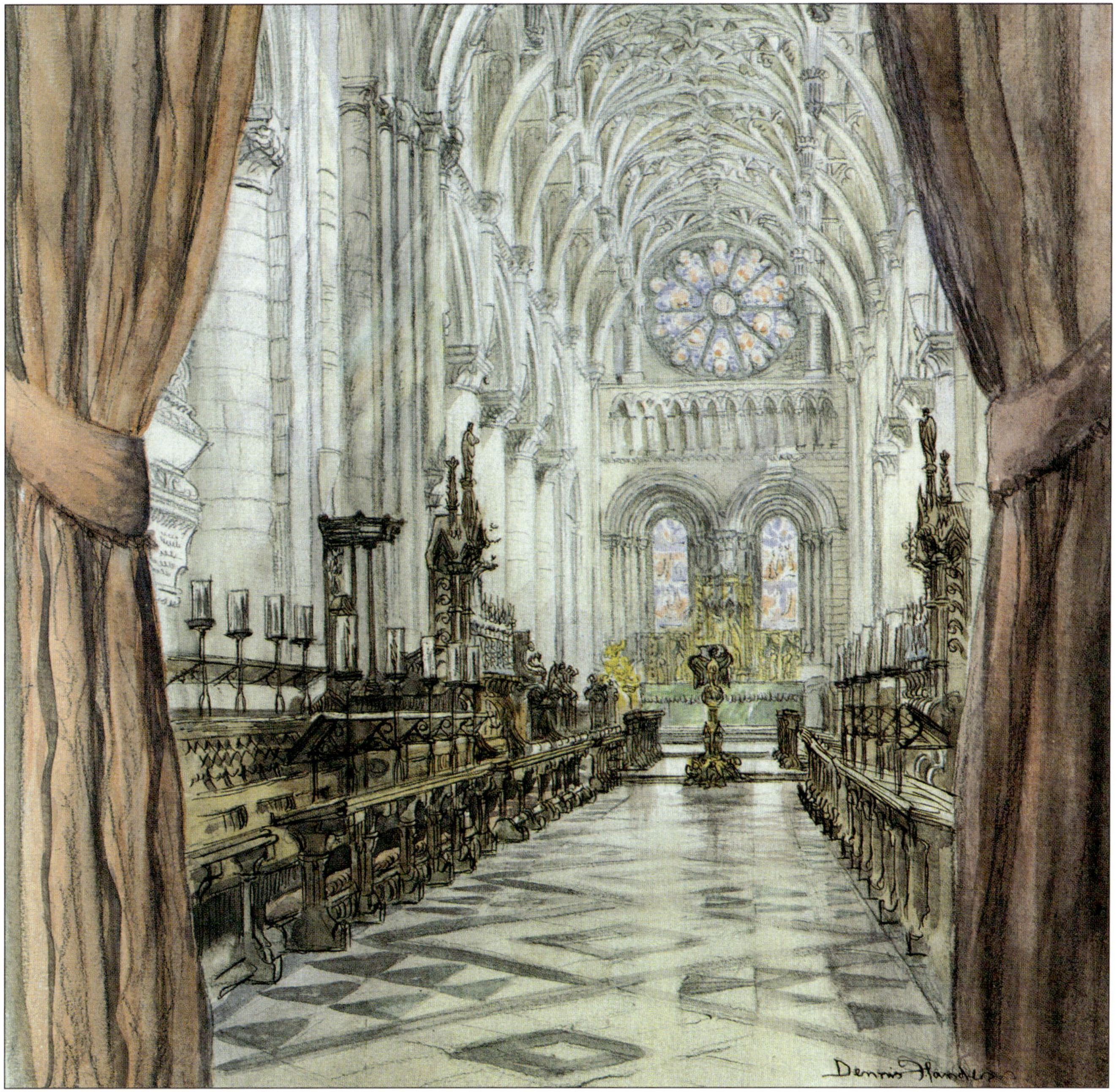

CORPUS CHRISTI COLLEGE

James Porteous Wood, RSW

The Front Quad

This is the only painting in the book that is *not* attributable to a member of the Royal Watercolour Society. James Porteous Wood is a Scotsman, and in 1945 became the youngest member to be elected to the Royal Scottish Watercolour Society.

He was a wartime buddy of another of our featured artists, Dennis Flanders. They were stationed at Catterick, and whenever they could get a 48-hour pass they would cycle to paint the scenery of the Yorkshire Dales.

James has, since retirement, become a full-time artist. Before this he was Artistic Director of Aspreys of Bond Street, and was commissioned by King Hassan of Morocco to produce a ten foot model of Mecca in solid silver and copper, inlaid with lapis lazuli.

Corpus Christi College was founded in 1517 by Richard Foxe, the Bishop of Winchester, who baptized Henry VIII and was blind. It was the last pre-Reformation College to be founded and, surprisingly, was secular, Bishop Foxe wishing to spread the teaching of Latin, Greek and Hebrew. It still has a fine reputation for teaching the classics.

The Pelican, the college's emblem taken from Bishop Foxe's coat of arms, can be seen surmounting the column containing the famous sundial. This was erected in 1581 by Charles Turnbull, a Fellow of the College. It celebrates Nicholas Kratzer, a Bavarian who was elected a Fellow of the College in 1517. He introduced horology – the science of measuring time – to England.

Jimmy now lives in Arisaig, overlooking the Inner Hebridean isle of Eigg. His wonderfully vivid view of the Corpus Christi Front Quad and its pelican sundial was painted from the first floor of the 16th century library, which has a splendid collection of 10th century manuscripts, and early printed books from the 15th century.

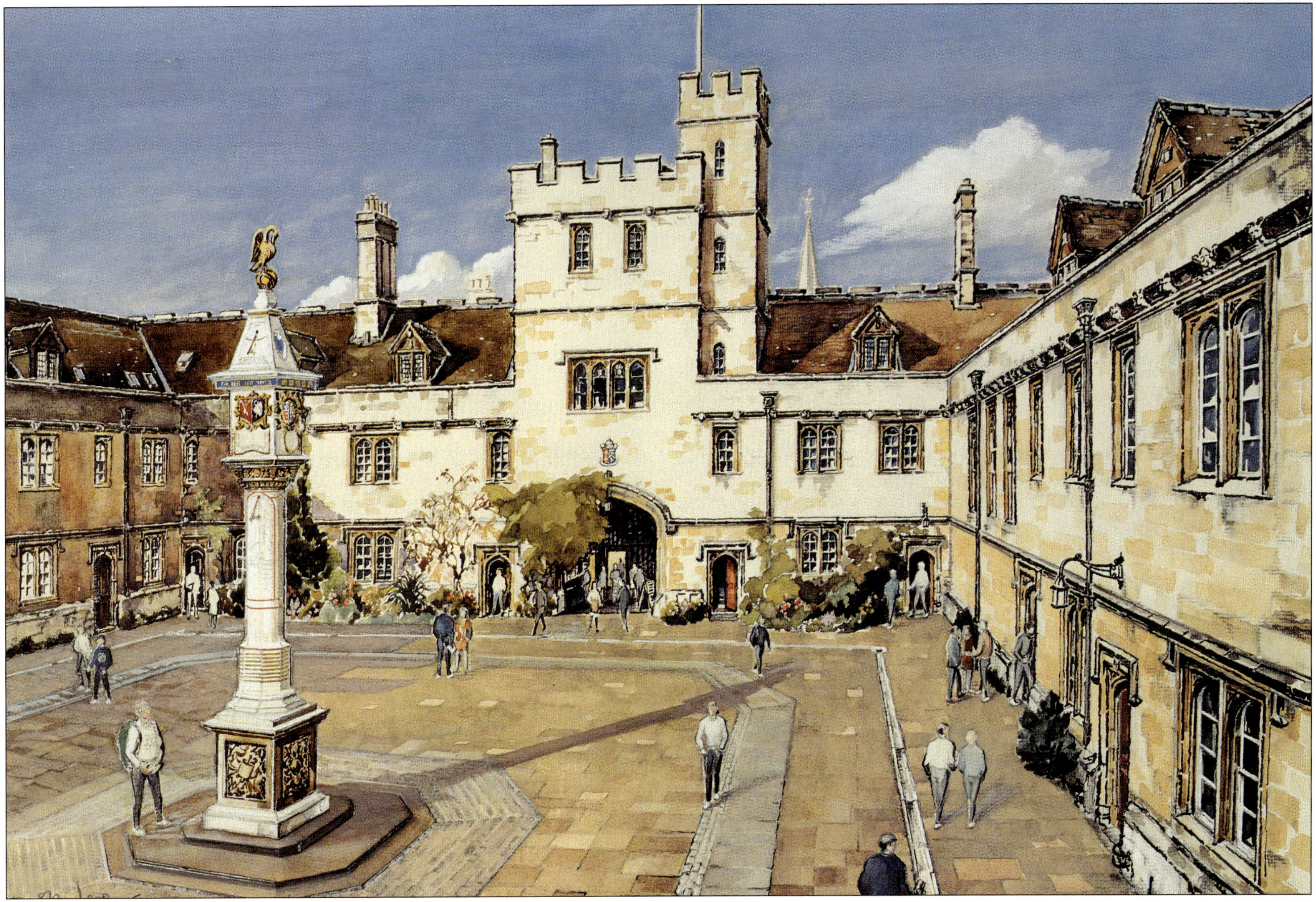

EXETER COLLEGE

Ken Howard

Front Quadrangle and Chapel

Three older colleges – Balliol, Merton and University – have a long-running dispute about which is the oldest. There is no dispute, however, over the fact that Exeter is the fourth oldest. It was founded in 1314 by Walter de Stapledon, Bishop of Exeter, and was governed for more than 500 years by a fairly large body of west country clergymen.

In the mid-19th century the wind of change swept through Oxford, and in 1856 Exeter introduced new statutes which opened it up to wider geographical and secular influence.

In more recent times Exeter has been even more radical. In 1993 it became the first of the former all-male colleges at either Oxford or Cambridge to elect a woman as its head – Marilyn Butler, Professor of English Literature at Cambridge.

The omnipresent chapel, completed in 1859, was the work of George Gilbert Scott. Its design was based on that of Sainte-Chapelle in Paris. In the chapel hangs a wonderful tapestry designed by Edward Burne-Jones, and executed by William Morris, who were both contemporaries at Exeter in the 1850s and leading members of the romantic pre-Raphaelite movement.

Ken Howard was greatly exercised in getting a workable perspective of the chapel in the context of its impressive dominance of the Front Quadrangle.

Equally impressive was the hospitality he received from the college and its Domestic Bursar, Susan Marshall. During his four-night stay he attended chapel in the evening and dined at High Table, giving him a flavour of university life which he himself had never experienced at first-hand.

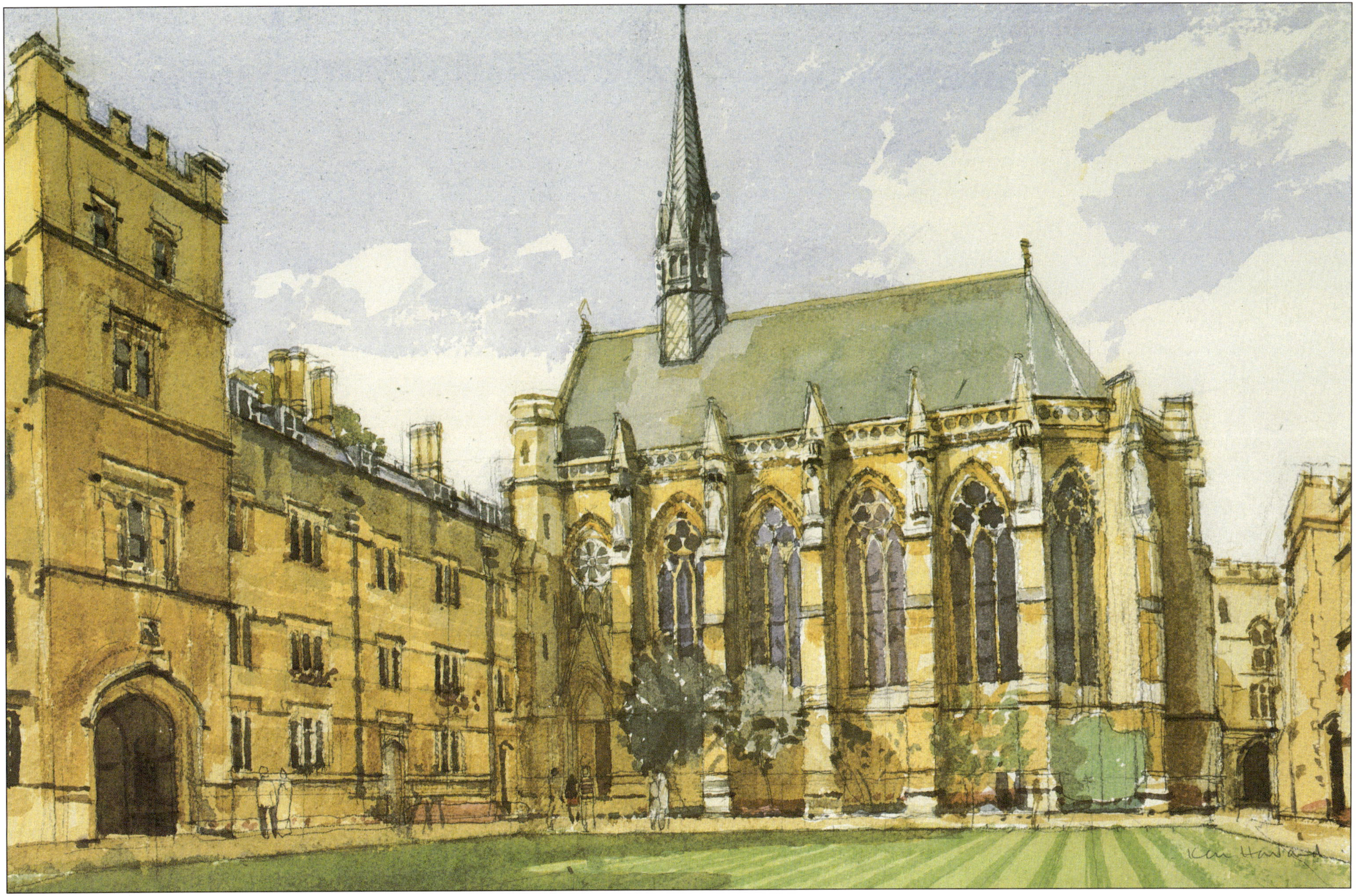

EXETER COLLEGE

Ken Howard

The Broad Street Front

When Christopher Wren built the Sheldonian Theatre in 1669 he commissioned William Byrd, the Oxford stonemason, to carve fourteen stone heads to stand in front of the building in Broad Street.

Nobody knows for certain what the heads represent, whether gods, wisemen or emperors. They were replaced in 1868 by poor copies made from an inferior version of the original Headington Freestone. They quickly became very badly worn and were in turn replaced in 1972 by heads commissioned from the Oxford sculptor Michael Black.

He managed to find eleven of the original 17th century heads which were haphazardly spread around gardens in Oxford. He used them as models for his new Clipsham stone heads.

Immediately to the right of the Sheldonian in Ken Howard's painting is the Old Ashmolean building, one of the finest examples of 17th century architecture in Oxford. It was designed by Thomas Wood and completed in 1683.

It was built to house the collection of *rarities* which the John Tradescants, father and son, had assembled, and which was made over to Elias Ashmole, who added it to his own collection of coins and other objects before handing them over to the University.

The museum moved to its present Beaumont Street location in 1852 and the old building now houses the Museum of the History of Science.

To the far right of the picture is the present Broad Street front of Exeter College which was started in the 1830s by H J Underwood, a local architect, and completed by George Gilbert Scott with the addition of the gateway and tower in 1859.

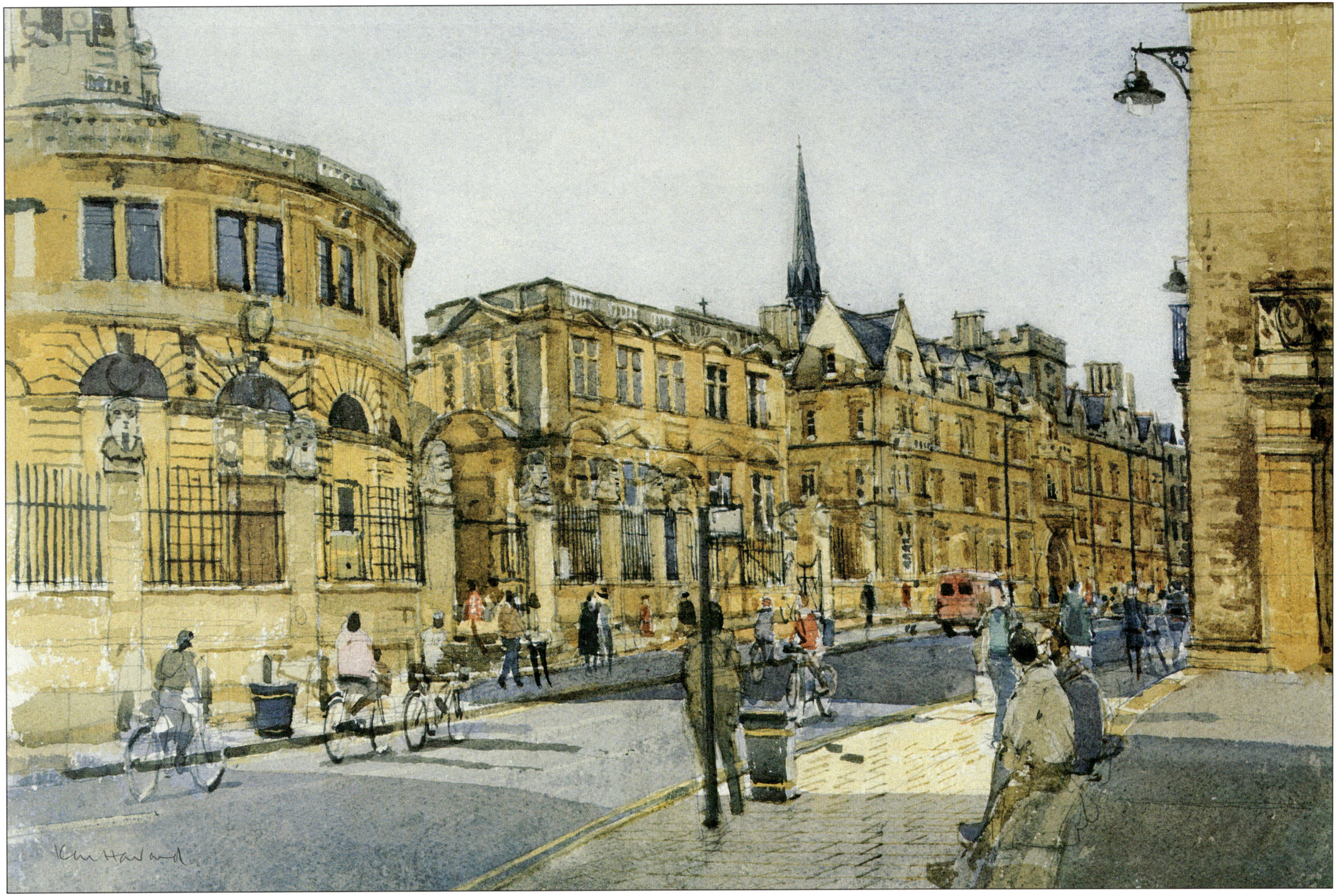

HERTFORD COLLEGE

Dennis Flanders

O.B. Quadrangle

One afternoon while chatting to me in his studio in Great Ormond Street, Dennis produced a large, dusty book on the work of his great mentor, Hanslip Fletcher. This was published in 1910 and contained pencil and ink drawings.

One in particular was a wonderful view of Oxford, incorporating the Radcliffe Camera, All Souls, and St Mary the Virgin, viewed from the third floor of Hertford College across the main quad.

"I would love to repeat that view as a watercolour painting," Dennis enthused. As a result, I contacted Roger Van Noorden, a Fellow and acting Bursar of Hertford College, who obtained permission from the governing body of the college for us to include Hertford in our alumni project.

Our first task was to locate the exact room from which Hanslip Fletcher had made his original drawing. This took some time as Dennis had to take frequent brief rests because of his emphysema.

We finally found the historic room. Dennis was delighted when Roger Van Noorden said he could take up residence in that very room after the end of the week because the students were going down for the long vacation. It was mid-June.

The view across the main quad, officially called the O.B. Quad (Old Buildings), so captivated Dennis that he produced a second drawing by moonlight, which he later issued as a Christmas card.

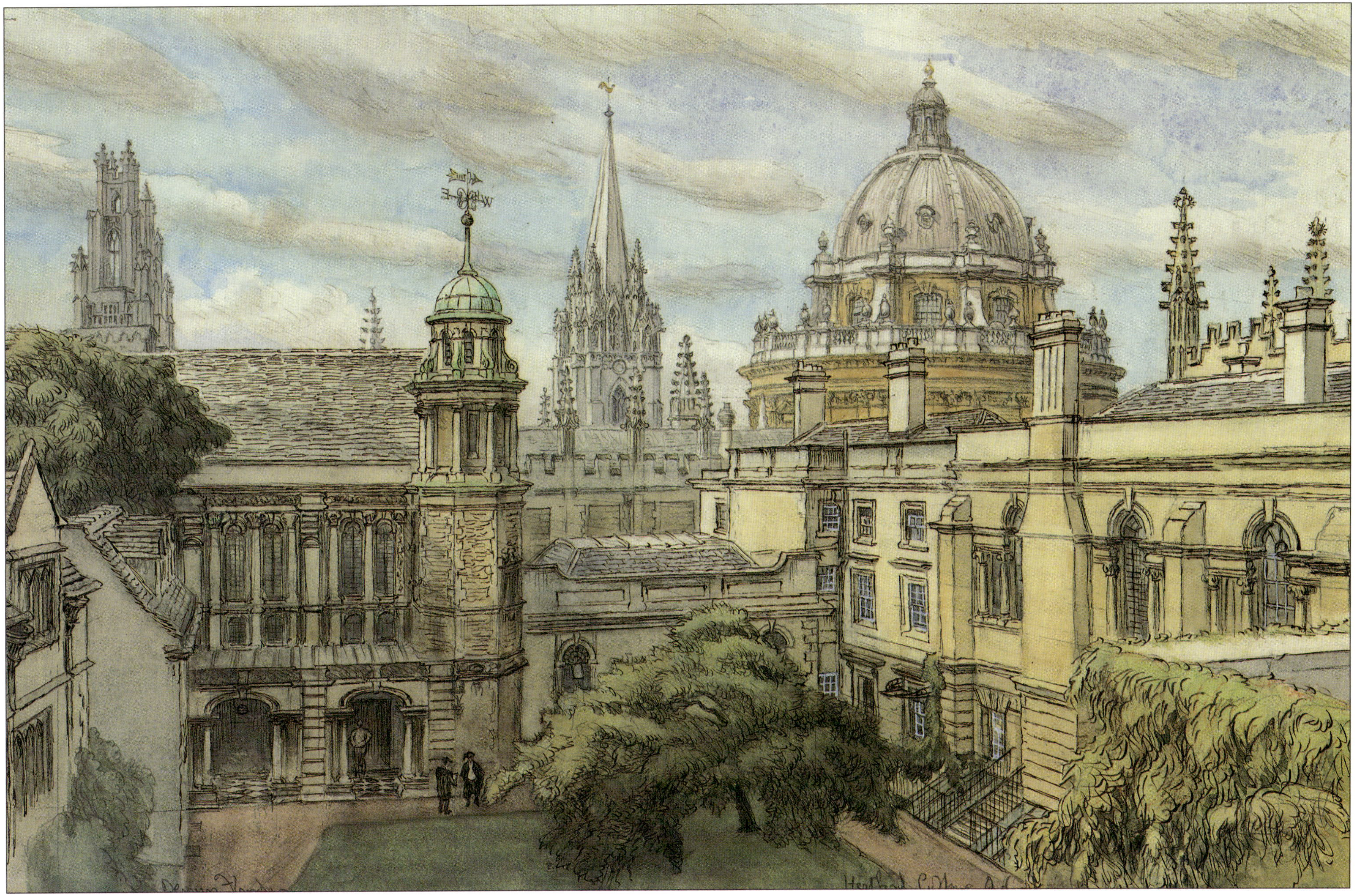

HERTFORD COLLEGE

Dennis Flanders

Bridge of Sighs

Originally founded as Hart Hall in 1283, it became Hertford College in 1740 but closed in 1818 due to lack of endowments, and the site was occupied by Magdalen Hall (1822-1874). In 1874 a noted banker, T C Baring, provided a generous endowment which effected the re-founding of Hertford College.

Dennis Flanders stayed for a week as a guest of Hertford College, and produced his second Hertford picture featuring the Bridge of Sighs, looking towards the Sheldonian Theatre.

The bridge linking the two newer parts of Hertford College was designed by Sir Thomas Jackson and completed in 1914. It is one of the landmarks of Oxford and was featured, along with other parts of the College, in the acclaimed television version of Evelyn Waugh's *Brideshead Revisited.* Waugh was himself an undergraduate at Hertford in the 1920s.

Dennis was most excited by this view because he witnessed the annual Encaenia Procession, the honorary degree ceremony whose adherents wear vivid scarlet gowns. This he incorporated into the picture.

He had just one complaint: "There were all these damn television people getting in my way." What in fact he had witnessed was the filming of an episode of *Morse*! His mentor, Hanslip Fletcher, would have been proud of his single-minded dedication, even in the face of Mammon and an art form that neither of them recognised. Dennis rarely watched television.

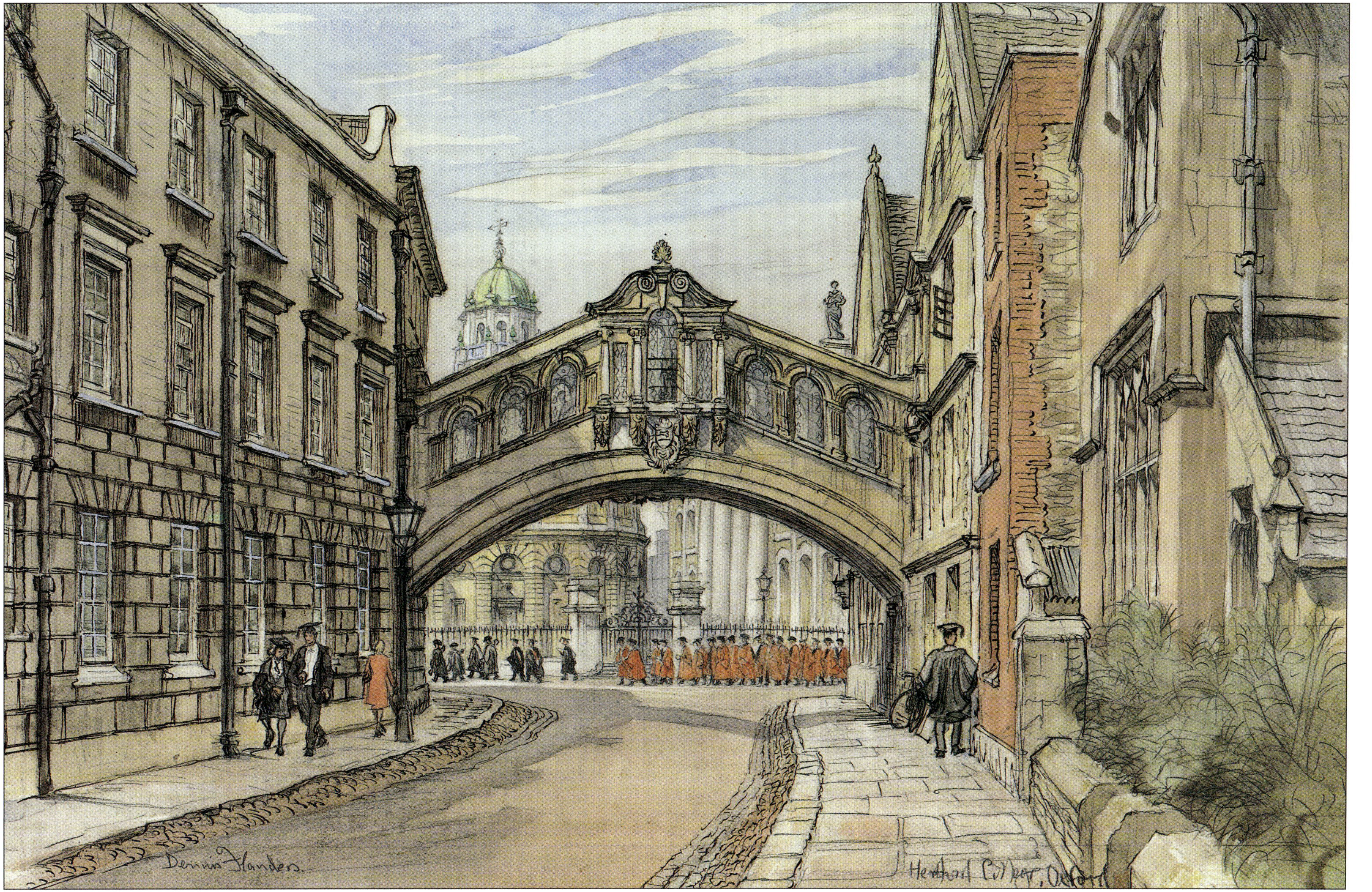
Dennis Flanders.
Hertford College, Oxford

JESUS COLLEGE

Ken Howard

The Turl Street Front

The painting of the Turl Street Front shows the oldest surviving part of Jesus College, the 16th century south front, although the tower over the entrance was added in 1854.

Ken Howard felt that this view was best captured in early spring before the wonderful plane tree in the foreground completely obliterated the front of the college. A winter view would have been too stark. Also, Ken's wonderful use of light, his trademark, so to speak, is beautifully demonstrated in this picture.

Jesus College has been associated with Wales since its foundation by Queen Elizabeth I in 1571 at the petition of Hugh Price, Treasurer of St David's Cathedral. He provided its first endowments, while the Queen provided the site, buildings and property of White Hall, a redundant academic hall. In fact it is the only Oxford College to date from the Elizabethan period.

Distinguished members of Jesus this century include T E Lawrence (Lawrence of Arabia), and former Prime Minister, Harold Wilson. In the ante chapel is a sightless bust of T E Lawrence, and the college also possesses his campaign notebooks.

Sir John Habakkuk, whose distinguished Principalship of the college extended from 1967 to 1984, was Vice-Chancellor of the University from 1973-1977. His successor as Principal, Sir Peter North, was also Vice-Chancellor of the University from 1993-1997.

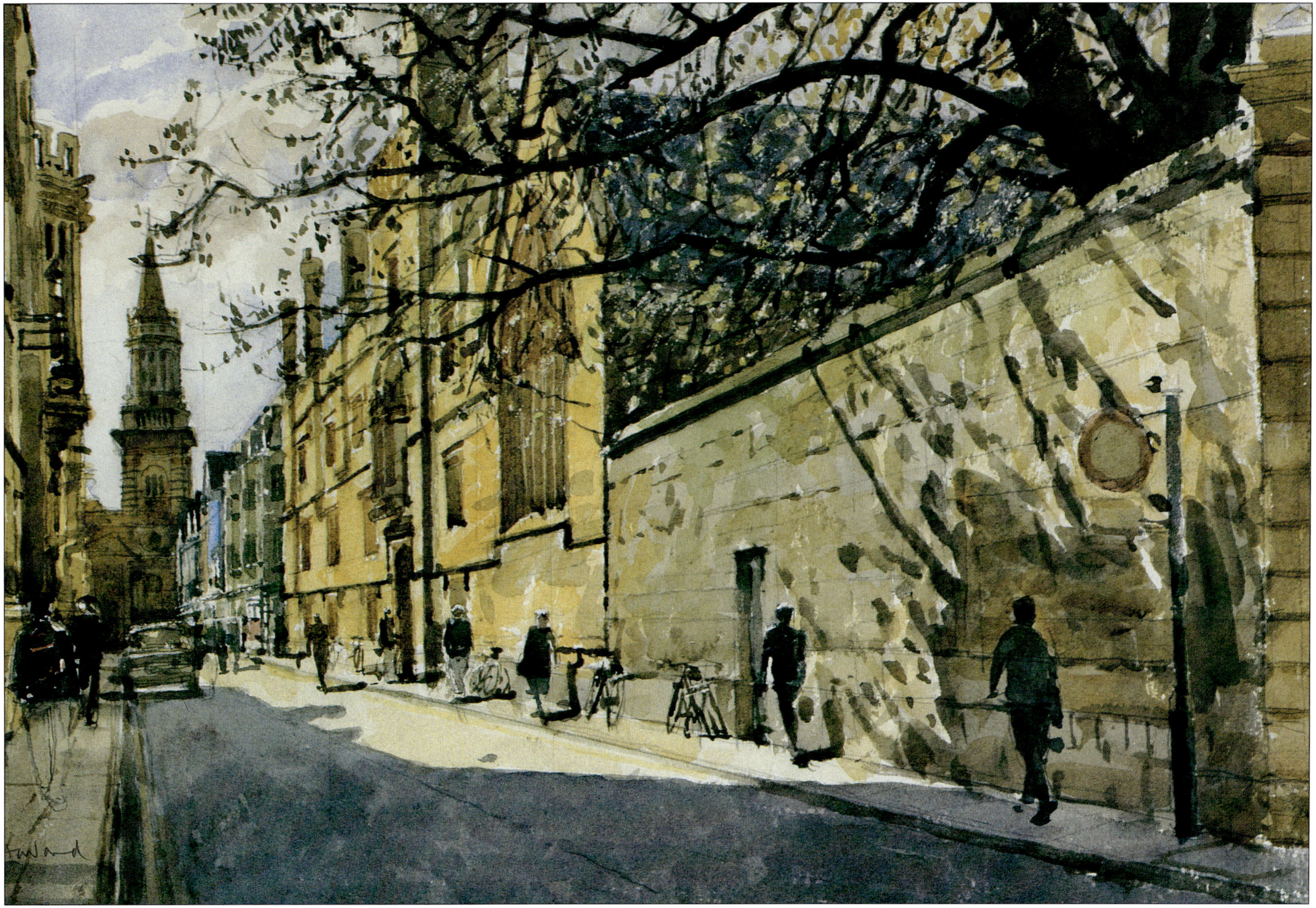

JESUS COLLEGE

Dennis Flanders

First Quadrangle

The First Quadrangle dates from the 17th century and contains the Hall, Chapel and Principal's lodgings. The Hall is situated to the right of the passageway in Dennis Flanders's very pretty painting, and further to the right is the shellhood entrance to the Principal's lodging.

In the Hall there hangs, in pride of place above High Table, a remarkable full-length portrait of Queen Elizabeth I by Nicholas Hilliard (1537-1619) – and thereby hangs a remarkable tale.

The painting, given to the college by Dr James Jeffreys, brother of the notorious "hanging" Judge Jeffreys, mouldered away for centuries in a dark corner of the Fellows' Library, completely unnoticed and unremarked. It had mainly, in the 17th century, been over-painted and was thought to be a later copy of some unknown contemporary painting and of little value. It was in effect a palimpsest.

Then in 1994 the art expert, Alec Cobb, was commissioned to clean the college portraits, including the Charles I portrait by Van Dyck. The Fellows' Library Elizabeth was not on his list but Mr Cobb noticed it and was curious. He thought the picture looked interesting and was given permission to bear it away for closer inspection.

After cleaning a section of the painting and submitting it to experts at Christies and Sotheby's, it was agreed that it was certainly the work of Nicholas Hilliard, best known for his execution of portrait miniatures. The provenance of the painting was further confirmed by Sir Roy Strong, an acknowledged expert on the paintings of Hilliard.

The over-painting was painstakingly removed, and what had been a forlorn picture in a corner was elevated to the status of a national treasure.

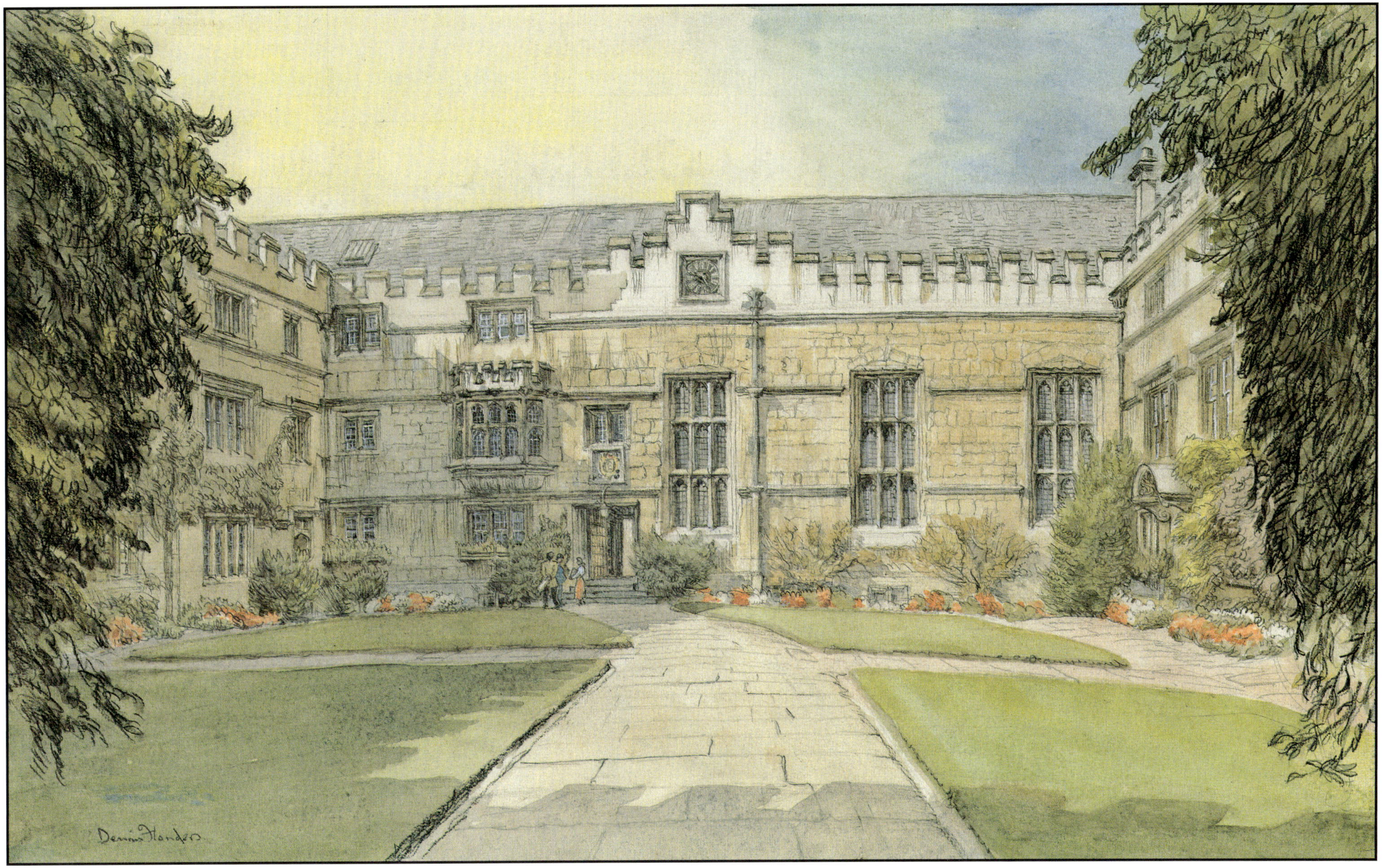
Dennis Flanders

KEBLE COLLEGE

Dennis Flanders

Liddon Quad

Keble College was founded in 1868 by public subscription as a memorial to John Keble, founder of the Oxford Movement.

William Butterfield was hired as architect and his red-brick masterpiece has caused controversy ever since. The new college was unlike any other in Oxford with its idiosyncratic use of bricks of different colours. You either love it or loathe it, according to your taste. John Betjeman loved it.

Butterfield's masterpiece has, as its crowning glory, the Chapel, which is given even greater prominence by his decision to sink the central part of the Liddon Quadrangle.

The interior of the Chapel is decorated with mosaics illustrating events from the Old and New Testaments, and in the side chapel hangs William Holman Hunt's painting, *The Light of the World*. There are two other versions of this picture but Keble's is the first and the one most fully Hunt's work.

Air Commodore Lovett, the Bursar at Keble, offered to take me to the top of the chapel tower because it afforded one of the highest viewing points in Oxford... vertigo caused me to decline.

Another notable innovation associated with Keble was the decision in 1871 to issue its own stamps for use on letters or messages delivered within the centre of Oxford. Seven other Oxford colleges followed Keble's lead. The postmaster general, however, objected to this backdoor privatisation and in 1886 the use of college stamps ceased.

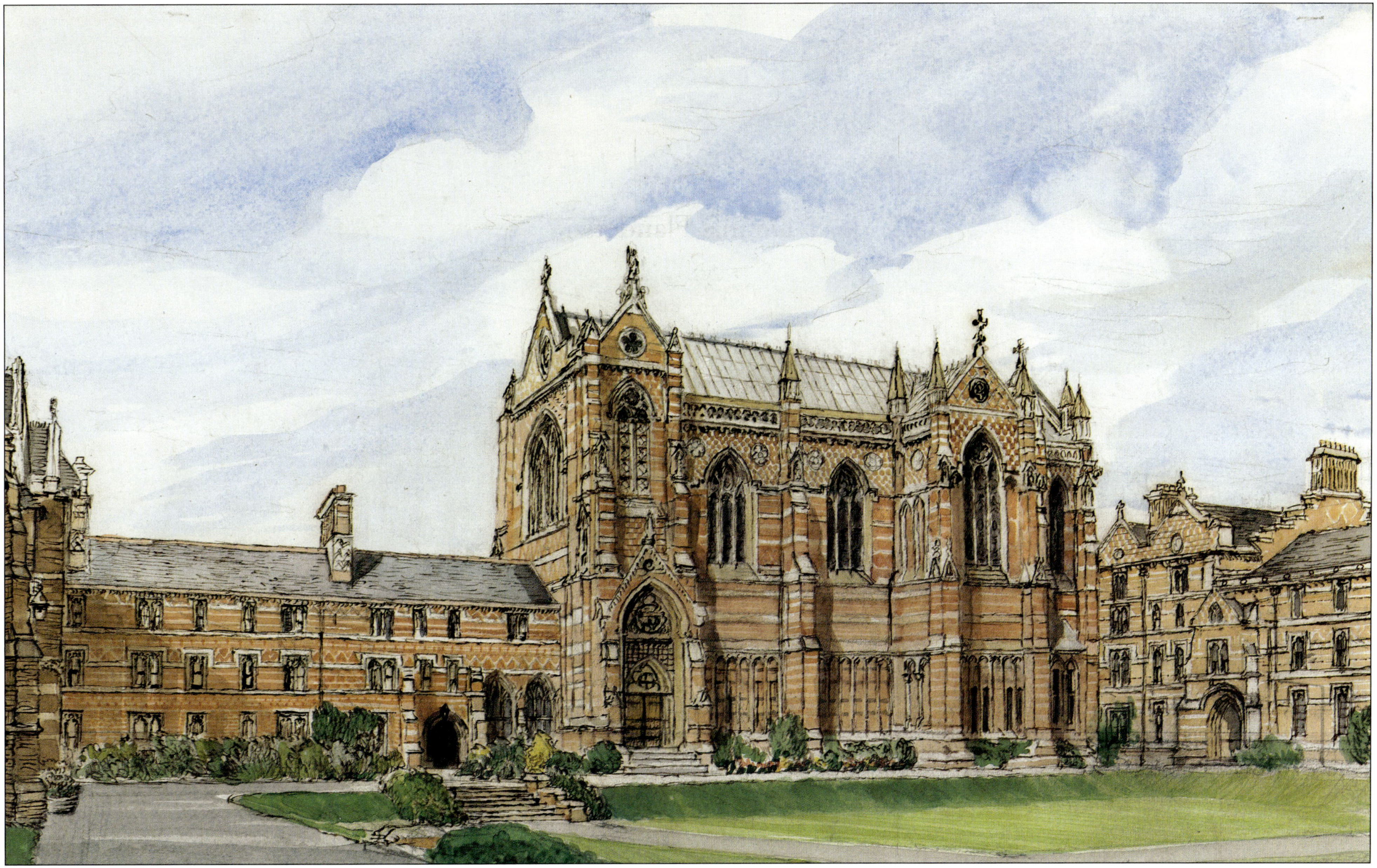

LADY MARGARET HALL

Dennis Roxby Bott

Talbot Hall and Quad

Women were not allowed into the wholly-male preserve of Oxford University until the first women's residential hall was founded in 1878 by Elizabeth Wordsworth, daughter of the Bishop of Lincoln and a great-niece of the poet.

She named the college after Lady Margaret Beaufort, Countess of Richmond and mother of Henry VII. Lady Margaret was a great patron of learning and a benefactress to both Oxford and Cambridge. In fact, she founded two Cambridge colleges – St John's and Christs.

The first chairman of the Lady Margaret Hall council was Edward Talbot, Warden of Keble, who ensured that only members of the Church of England could be admitted to the college. The last religious restrictions were not removed until 1968.

Initially, women could not become members of the University, being given only diplomas until 1920 when they were given degree status. In 1979 men were admitted to Lady Margaret Hall.

In 1893 an eight-acre tract of land running from Norham Gardens down to the river Cherwell was purchased from St John's College. The first buildings on it were designed by Sir Reginald Blomfield and erected between 1896 and 1915 in pleasing red brick. They were named Wordsworth, Talbot and Lodge.

Dennis was keen to undertake the Lady Margaret Hall project because his sister was a graduate of the college when it was still an all-ladies' college. The attractive arch frames his view of the Quad and Talbot Hall beautifully.

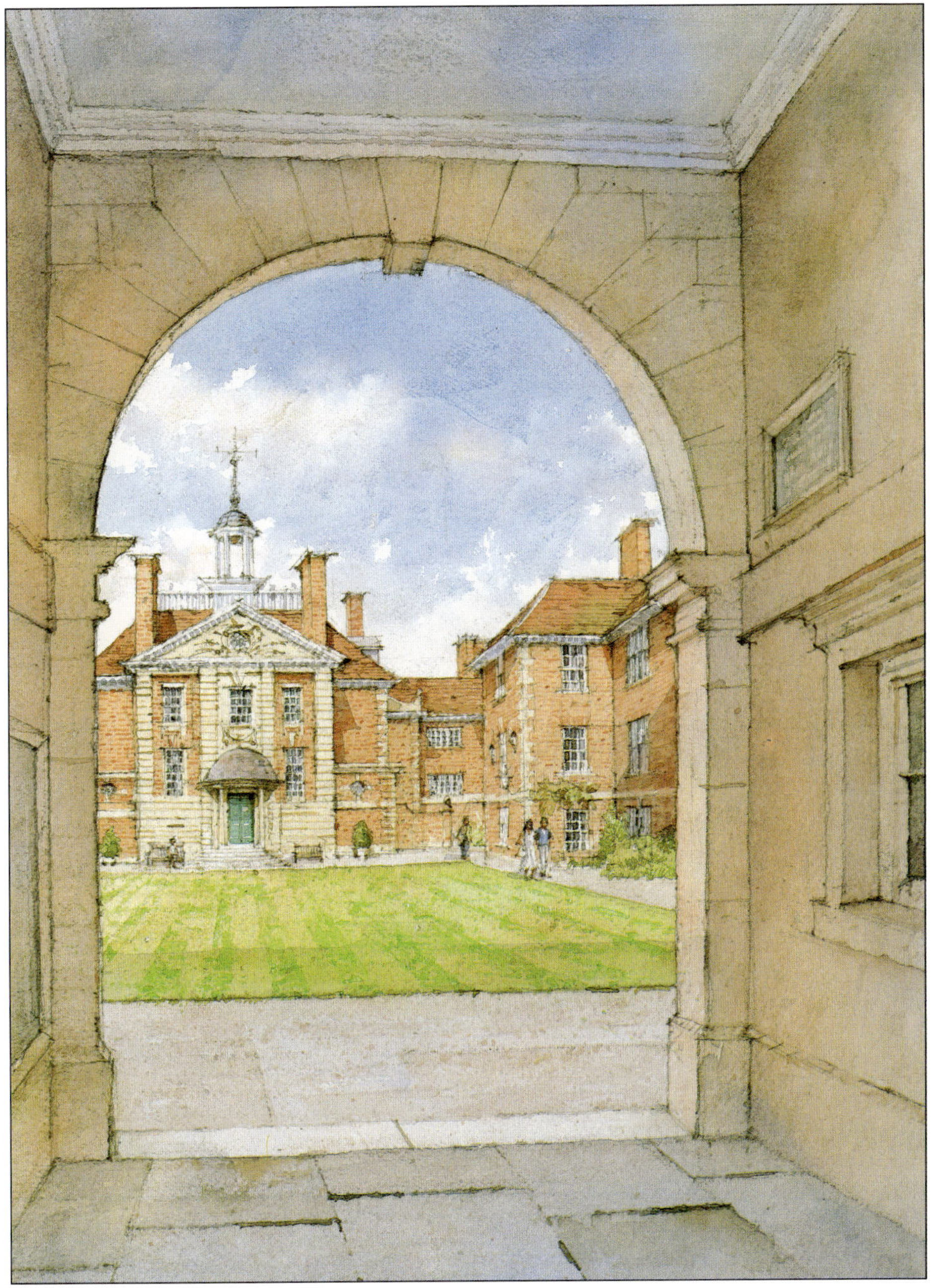

LINCOLN COLLEGE

Jane Carpanini

Front Quad

Founded in 1427 by the Bishop of Lincoln, Richard Fleming, the College was somewhat impecunious in the early years, so there was little money for modernization. Although not appreciated at the time, this proved to be of great benefit because today the college retains much of its mediaeval architecture, particularly some of the interiors.

The Front Quad dates from 1437, and contains the hall, which has a 15th century timbered roof with its original smoke louvres still in position.

Lincoln's most influential scholar is John Wesley, who made the college the cradle of Methodism. From 1726 until 1735 he occupied rooms in Chapel Quad, during which time the Holy Club was set up. He departed for Georgia in the USA as a Missionary Chaplain in 1735. He remained a fellow until 1751 when he married.

The room where he gave his tutorials is in the south-east corner of the Front Quad. In 1926, to commemorate the 200th anniversary of Wesley's election to a fellowship, Methodists in America paid for 15th century linenfold panelling to be installed, together with 18th century furniture.

The Gatehouse entrance tower contains the Rector's office which, at the time Jane Carpanini undertook her painting in year 2000, was occupied by the distinguished educationist Dr Eric Anderson. He was just about to retire as Rector of Lincoln to return to Eton. He is the thirteenth former Headmaster of Eton to return as Provost.

Jane Carpanini reflected that when making a drawing of a mediaeval building such as Lincoln's Front Quad, one had to be careful to spot the subtle changes made over the centuries. The odd window being removed can result in the gaps between the remaining windows being uneven, which might not be obvious to the casual observer. Lincoln is a case in point.

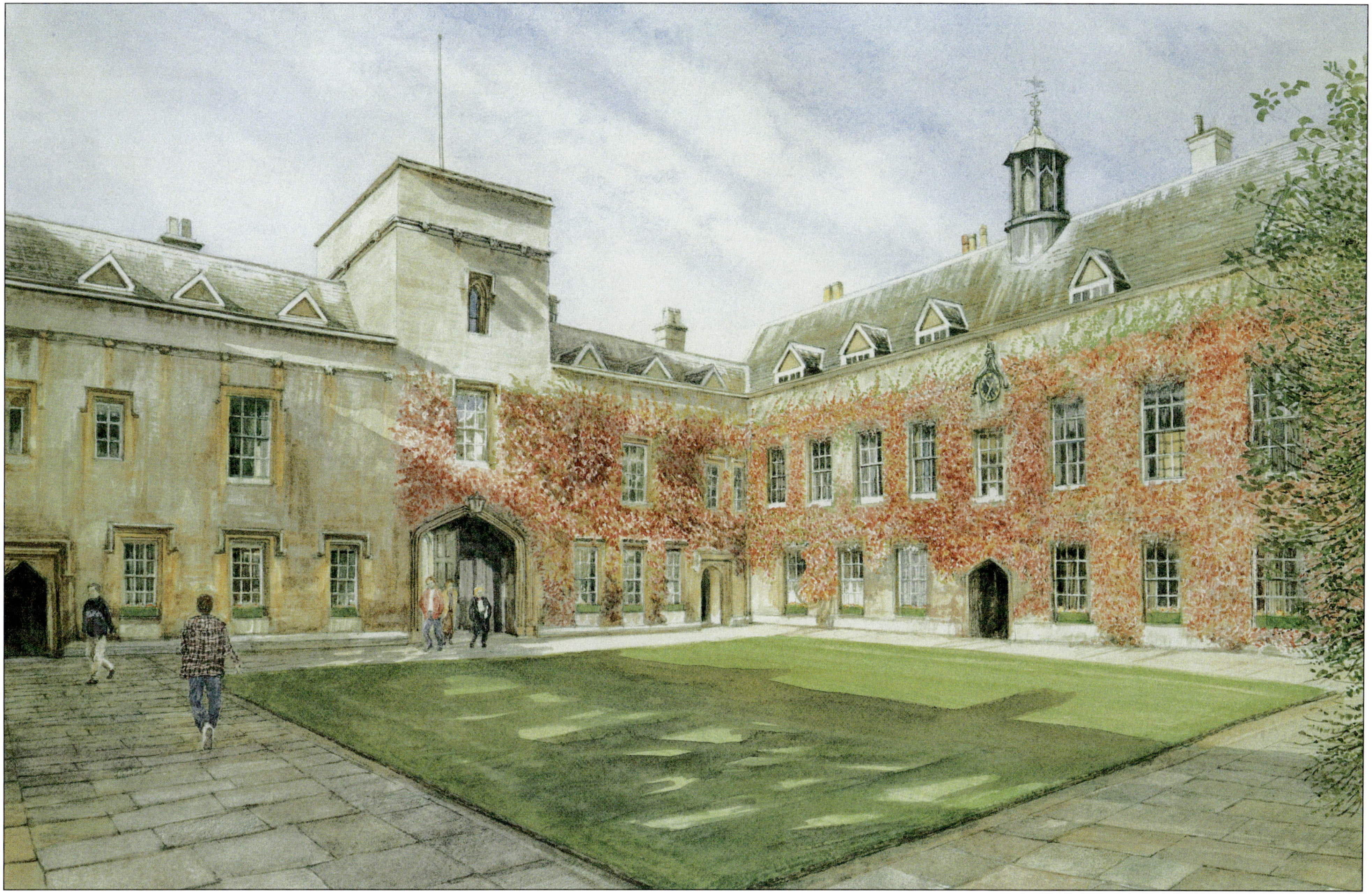

LINCOLN COLLEGE

Jane Carpanini

Turl Street

Lincoln straddles both sides of Turl Street including, on the west side, shops and the 15th century Mitre Hotel. The upper floors above all of these commercial tenancies have been converted into accommodation for students.

At the end of Turl Street can be seen one of Oxford's landmarks, All Saints Church, which was founded in the 12th century. The present building dates from 1720 and was the work of the great amateur architect, Henry Aldridge, Dean of Christ Church, and Nicholas Hawksmoor, a scholar and domestic clerk of Christopher Wren.

All Saints was, from the 19th century, the City Church. It is one of Oxford's most stylish buildings and completes the wonderful view of the High so beloved by artists. All Saints was declared redundant by the Church Commissioners and closed in 1971, and converted into Lincoln College Library in 1975.

John Radcliffe, who was one of Lincoln's most distinguished fellows (1670-1675) was a wealthy doctor, and physician to Queen Anne, whose benefactions named after him – the Radcliffe Camera, the Radcliffe Infirmary and the Radcliffe Observatory – adorn the City.

It seems odd, therefore, that the first benefaction from his large estate when he died in 1714 was to build the Radcliffe Quadrangle at University College as he intended. This was probably due to the fact that he was out of sympathy with Lincoln because they refused to dispense him from the obligation of taking Holy Orders, so forcing his resignation. In 1975, however, the trustees of his estate were more forgiving when they contributed generously to the conversion of All Saints Church into the College Library.

Jane Carpanini's timeless portrayal of Turl Street is little different from that which Turner painted nearly two hundred years ago. What has changed, however, is the street furniture – signs, entry restrictions etc – which now proliferates. Artistic licence has removed these ugly intrusions.

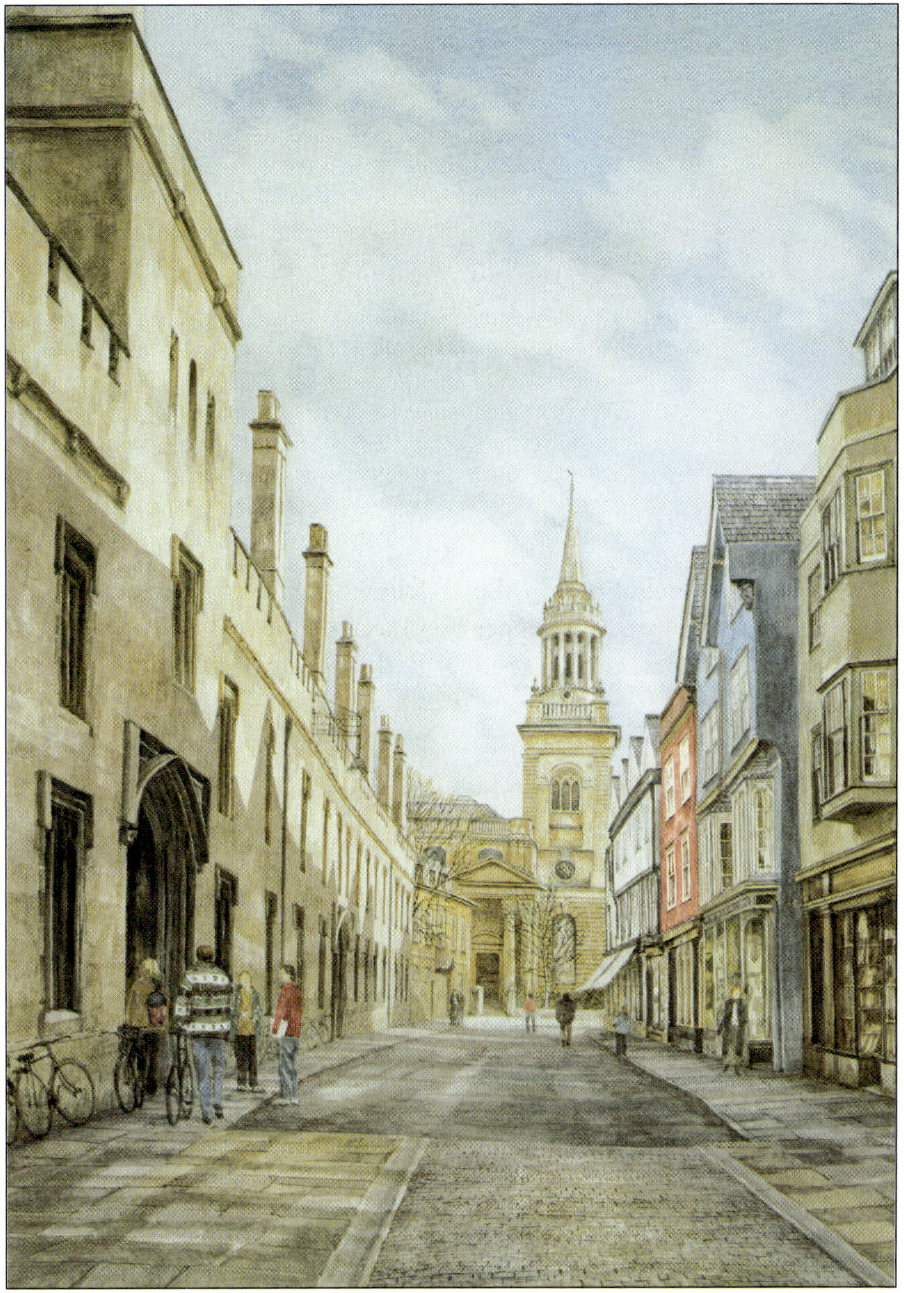

MAGDALEN COLLEGE

Dennis Flanders

View from the High

In June 1958, Dennis produced five watercolour drawings which appeared in the *Illustrated London News* to celebrate Magdalen's quin-centenary. In its editorial the magazine announced that the Duke of Windsor was among the 3,000 Old Members who were being invited to take part in the celebration on 12th June. There was to be a special Evensong service in the College Chapel, followed by a dinner and choral singing.

In late 1993, thirty-five years later, I approached the college authorities to see if they would be interested in reproducing two of the five original paintings. To this they readily agreed.

The two scenes represented are timeless and it is difficult to identify any noticeable changes except for the vehicles. The car and the perambulator are quite clearly of their time.

The Bell Tower of Magdalen College, which dominates the picture, is one of the outstanding landmarks of Oxford. It becomes the centre of world-wide attention on May morning at six o'clock when the thronging masses below listen to the choir on high sing a welcome to the coming summer.

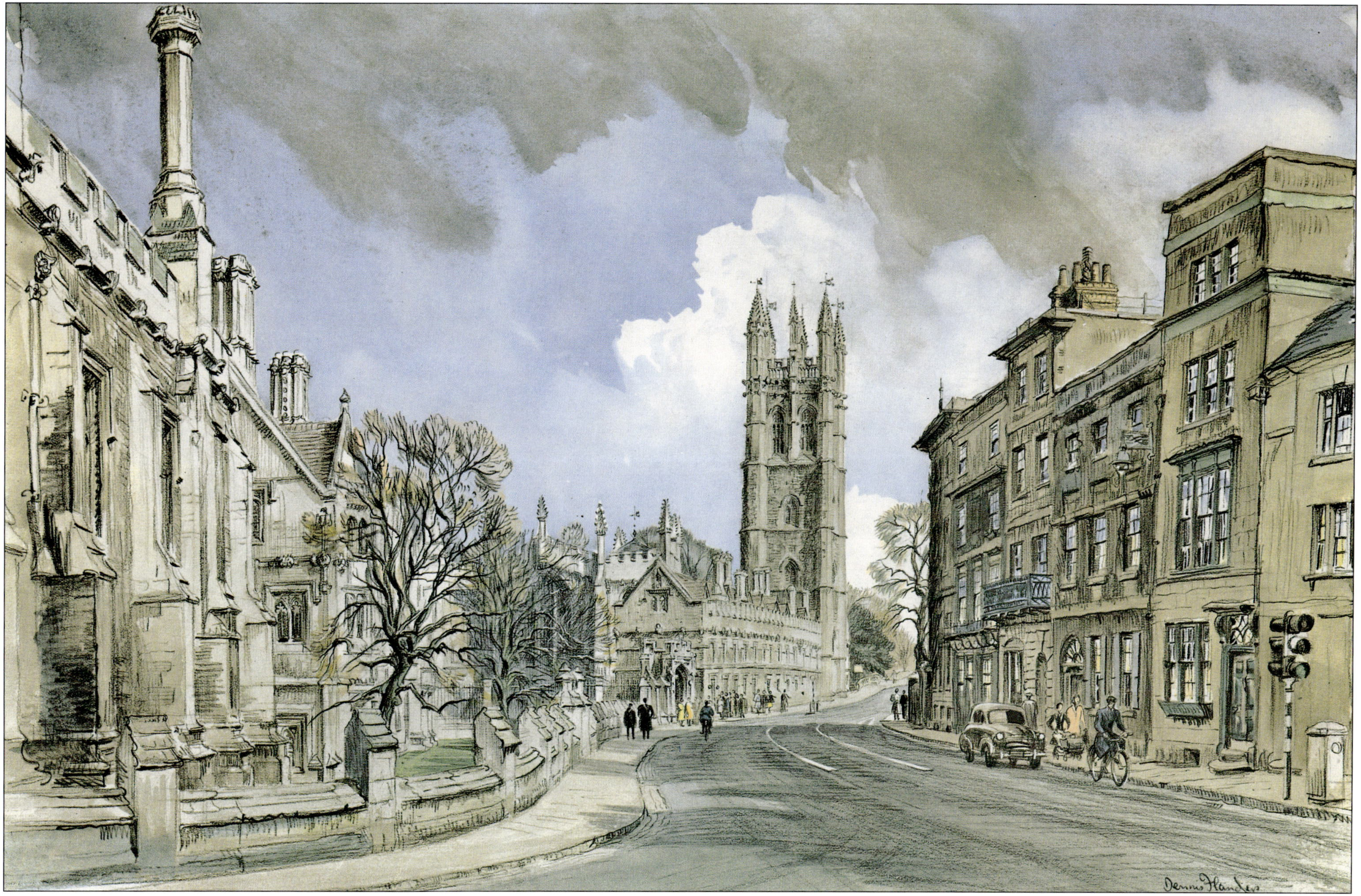
Dennis Flanders

MAGDALEN COLLEGE

Dennis Flanders

New Buildings

Magdalen College was founded in 1458 by William Waynflete, who became not only Bishop of Winchester but also, uniquely, Headmaster, successively, of both Eton and Winchester.

New Buildings was erected in 1733 and makes a wonderful Georgian contrast to the more mediaeval styles of the rest of Magdalen.

It was featured in the film *Shadowlands,* with Anthony Hopkins playing C S Lewis, who resided there for thirty years having been elected Fellow of Magdalen in 1925.

Many other literary and musical luminaries studied at Magdalen with varying degrees of success. Oscar Wilde gained a double first whereas John Betjeman was rusticated. Ivor Novello sang in the choir and Dudley Moore was an organ scholar.

The deer park adjoining New Buildings is the only one in Oxford and was first stocked in 1710. The deer are regularly culled, so venison is continually a feature of the college menu.

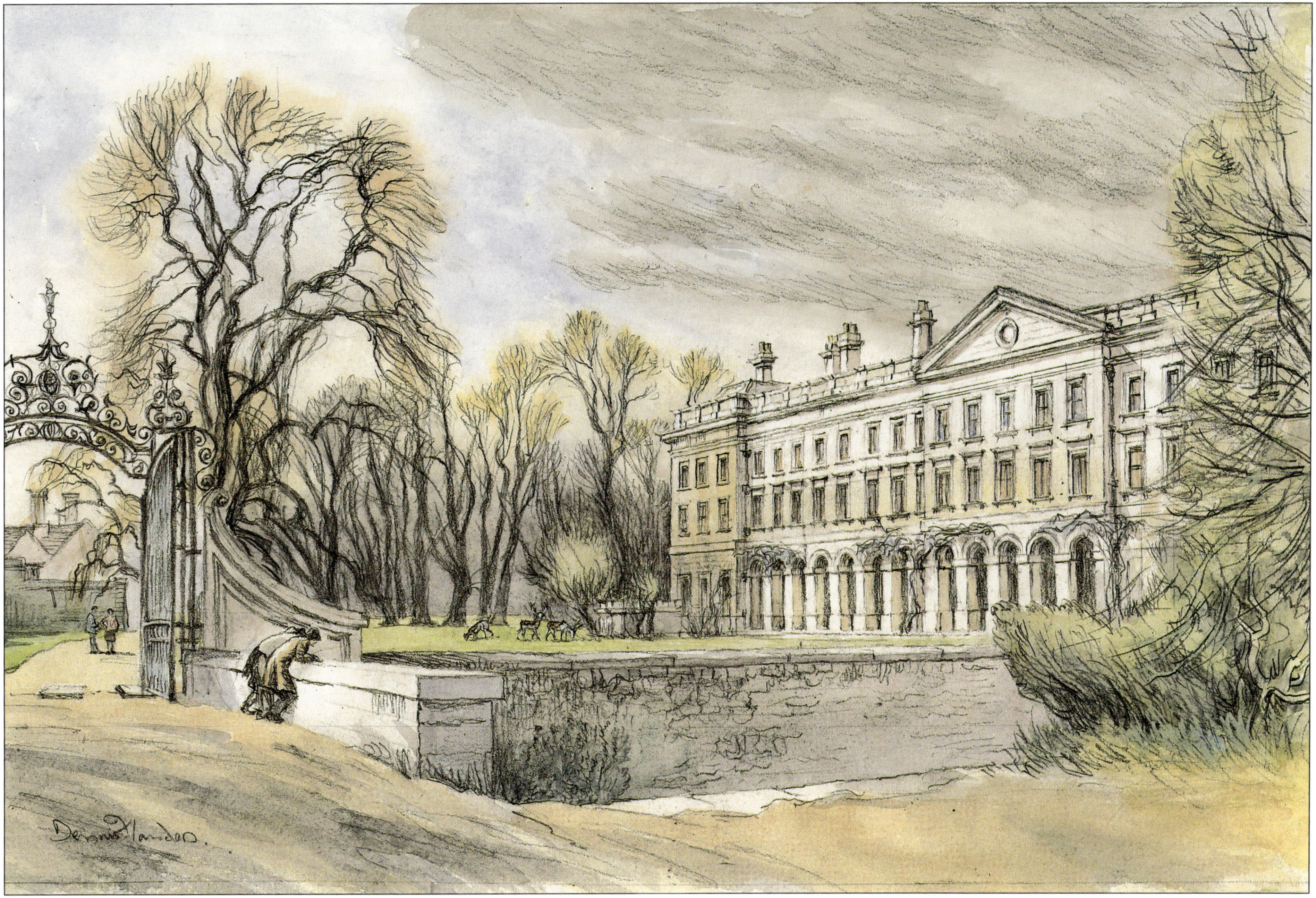
Dennis Flanders.

MANSFIELD COLLEGE

Dennis Roxby Bott

The Quad

Religious tests were abolished in 1871 and Oxford University was opened up to non-conformists. As a result, in 1886 Spring Hill Theological College in Birmingham decided to move to Oxford. It was renamed Mansfield College after the family who had originally founded Spring Hill in 1838.

The architect, Basil Champneys, designed the buildings for the new college in the best collegiate gothic style. It was meant to blend in with its Oxford setting; to become a seamless addition when completed in 1889.

The chapel on the right in Dennis's drawing has beautiful oak and stone carving, and its stained glass was designed by that successful pre-Raphaelite duo, William Morris and Edward Burne-Jones. The great organ was built by W G Vowles of Bristol and was a firm favourite of Dr Albert Schweitzer when he was at the College as Dale Lecturer in 1934.

The Hall and Senior Common Room are located to the right of the tower and Dennis was particularly fortunate with the weather when depicting this view. It was a beautiful, sunny day with the shadows laid out in precise detail. He was thus able to complete his painting with only one visit.

Initially, theological teaching and research were Mansfield's principal concerns, but now more than eighty per cent of its students are studying secular subjects.

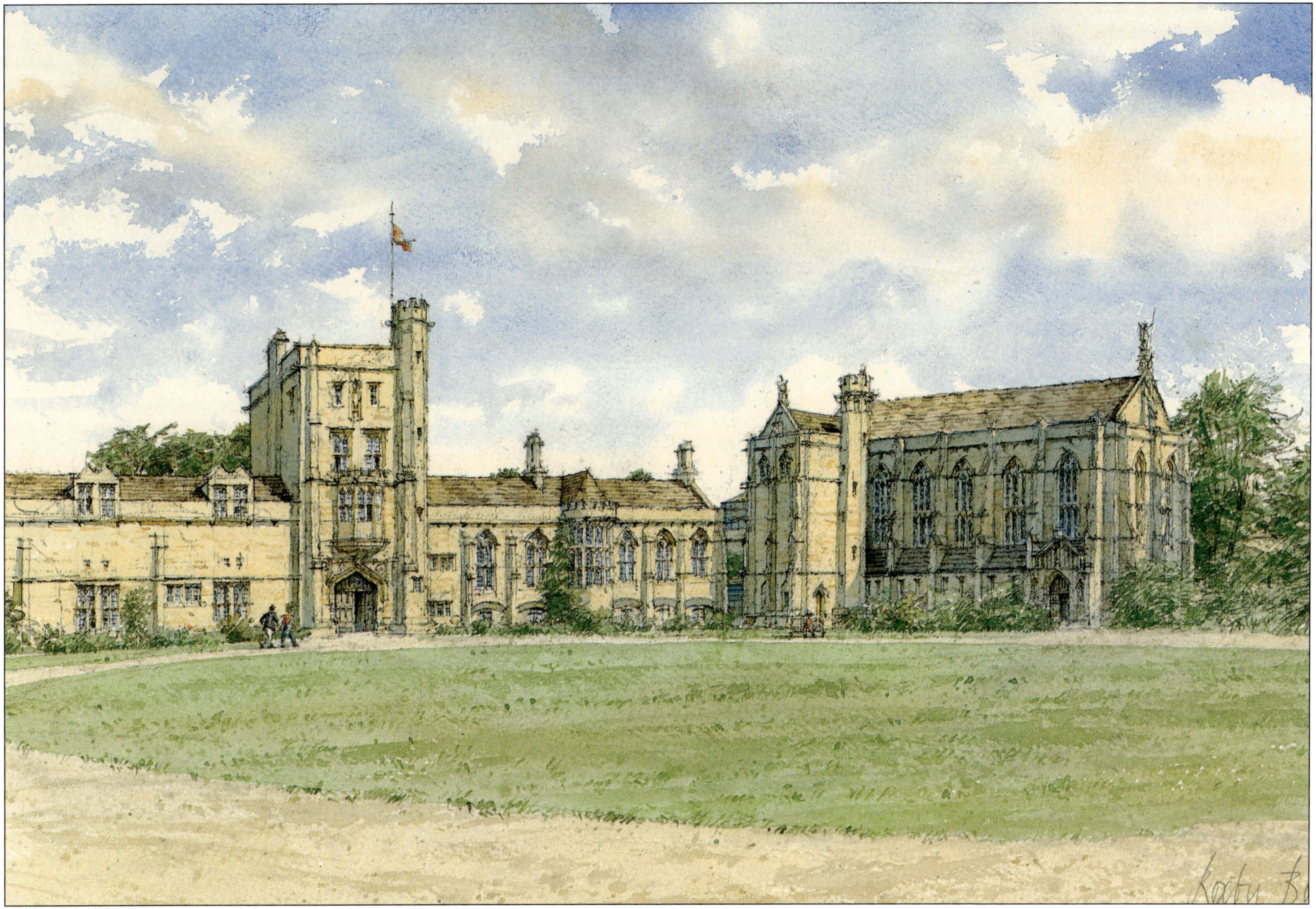

MERTON COLLEGE

John Doyle

Mob Quad

Merton still has a dispute with Balliol and University about which is the oldest college in Oxford and it depends on which basis judgment is made. If the criterion, however, is which college was first to have a resident student population, then Merton is the oldest.

It was founded in 1264 by Walter de Merton, later Bishop of Rochester, and was the model on which the first Cambridge college, Peterhouse, was founded by the Bishop of Ely in 1282. University and Balliol claim to have been founded in 1249 and 1263 respectively.

What is not in dispute, however, is that Mob Quad, which is the subject of John Doyle's painting opposite, is the oldest quad in Oxford. It also houses what is probably the oldest working library in the world, dating from 1371. Large dormer windows were added to the library in the 16th century in order to let in more light, candles being forbidden.

The old library is on the first floor of the range of buildings to the left in John Doyle's painting. On the ground floor is a more recent library for the use of students of history, classics and philosophy. While on the subject of libraries, Thomas Bodley, the founder of the University's Bodleian Library, was a Fellow of Merton and is buried in Merton Chapel.

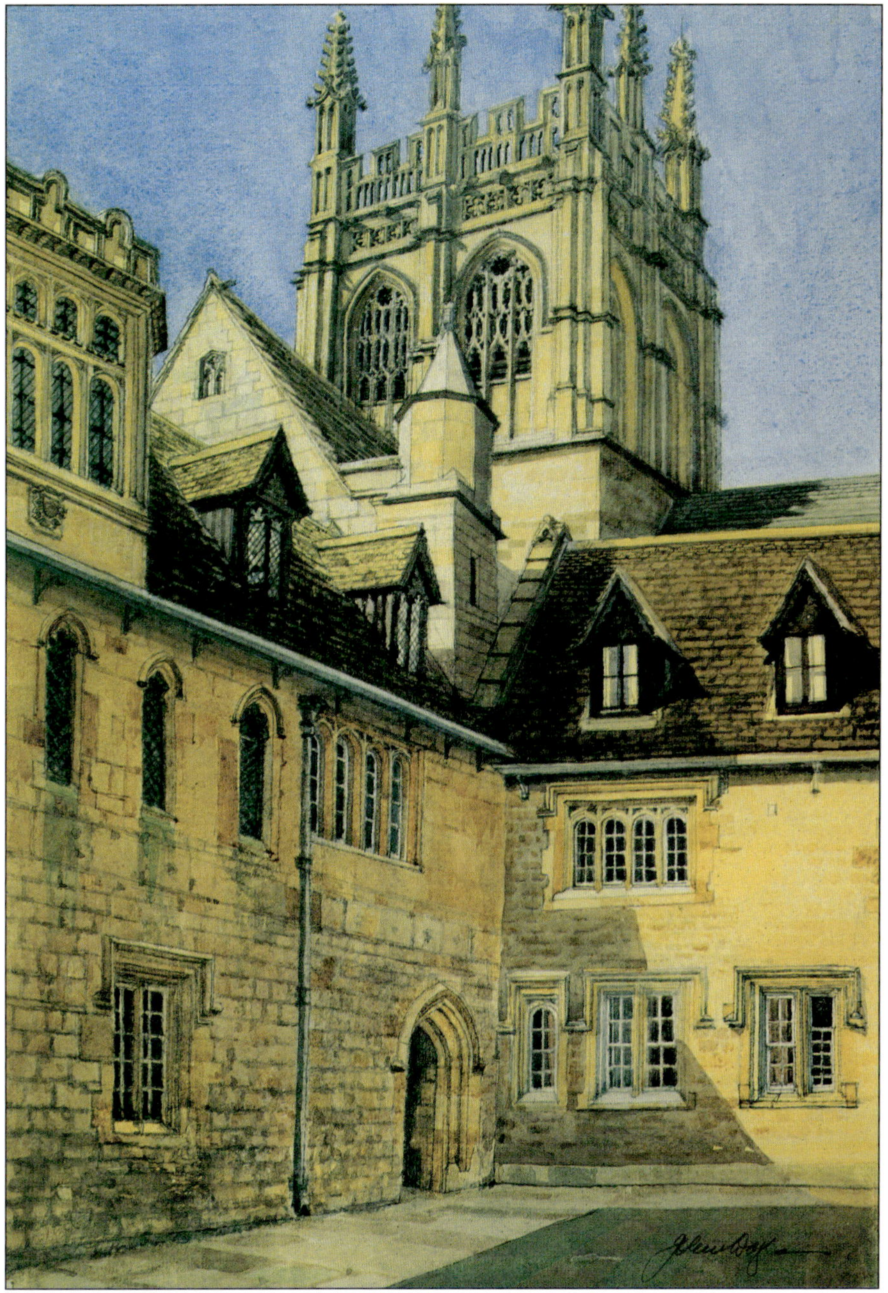

MERTON COLLEGE

John Doyle

Front Quad

Merton has an immense chapel, cathedral-like in size, with one of the most impressive towers in Oxford. Some of the glass in the Choir window is 13th century and is certainly the oldest of any Oxford college.

John Doyle, however, was keen to have a painting featuring the Great East window which has an oculus at its apex. This can be clearly seen in John's watercolour of the Front Quad. The oculus is the eye of the window resembling, in this case, a rose window – which it is not, because it does not stand alone. The tracery of the east window is 13th century but the glass is mainly 15th century. All eight bells date from 1680-1681.

To the left in the painting can be seen the fine 16th century porch tower whose steps lead past a magnificent 13th century door to the Hall, which was constructed in 1277.

The front quadrangle is unusual inasmuch as it is not symmetrical. The hall, which is opposite the college gateway, does not run parallel to the Merton Street front, but was probably in line with the original parish church which is no longer extant.

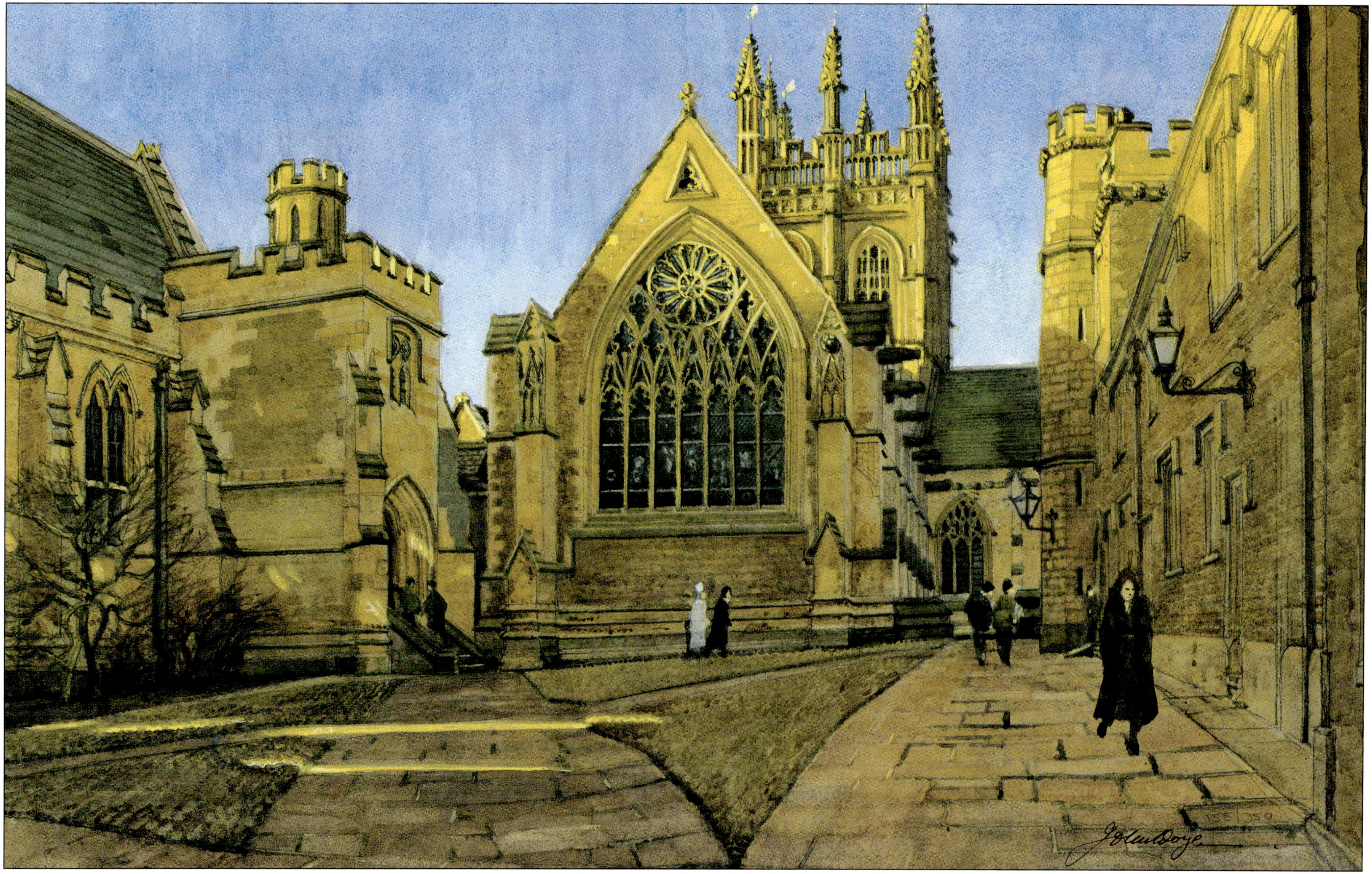

NEW COLLEGE

Dennis Flanders

The Great Quad

When founded in 1379, William of Wykeham's College, the seventh oldest in Oxford, was known as The St. Mary College of Winchester in Oxford. There was already, however, another college in Oxford dedicated to St. Mary – Oriel College. As a result, William of Wykeham's foundation became known as New College.

There are two main points of entry into New College. The original entrance into the Great Quad was down New College Lane. This is now the visitors' entrance where an admission fee is charged. The working entrance with Porter's Lodge is in Holywell Street.

Dennis was keen to produce a watercolour of the Great Quad which contained all the principal buildings essential to the communal life envisaged by the founder, including chapel, hall and library. It was the prototype quadrangle on which many subsequent foundations were based.

Dennis also wished to incorporate into the picture the fine bell tower, which was not quite visible from the vantage point at which he had positioned his stool and drawing-board.

With the assistance of the janitor, I spent a precarious hour or so clambering over the roofs and parapets of the Great Quad in order to photograph the bell tower rising above the chapel. This Dennis added to his painting with fine effect.

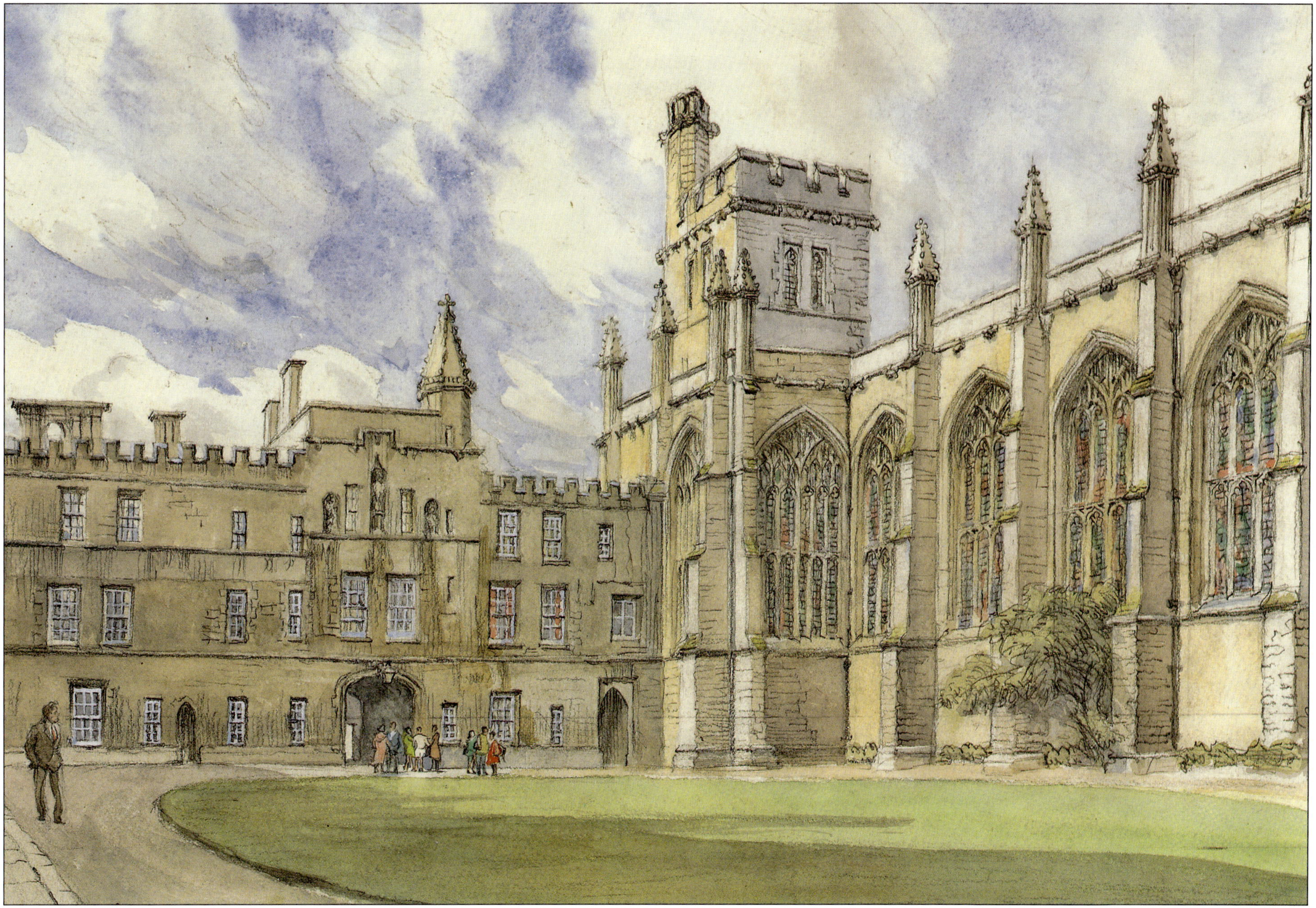

NEW COLLEGE

Dennis Flanders

Holywell Quadrangle

This represents both the newest and oldest part of New College. Three sides of Holywell Quadrangle were completed in 1896 and were the work of two architects, Sir George Gilbert Scott and Basil Champneys. Its fourth side, however, is formed by the 12th century City Wall, clearly visible on the right-hand side of the painting.

Since 1982, the Holywell entrance has been the one mainly used by students, and it contains the main Porter's Lodge at the base of the fine Robinson Tower. Because of the profusion of eminently drawable views available at New College, the Holywell Quadrangle is not often depicted by contemporary artists.

Dennis was keen to produce a watercolour to redress this unjustified imbalance, particularly as the quadrangle is now clearly the hub or axis of New College, as demonstrated by the great congregation of bicycles around the Porter's Lodge.

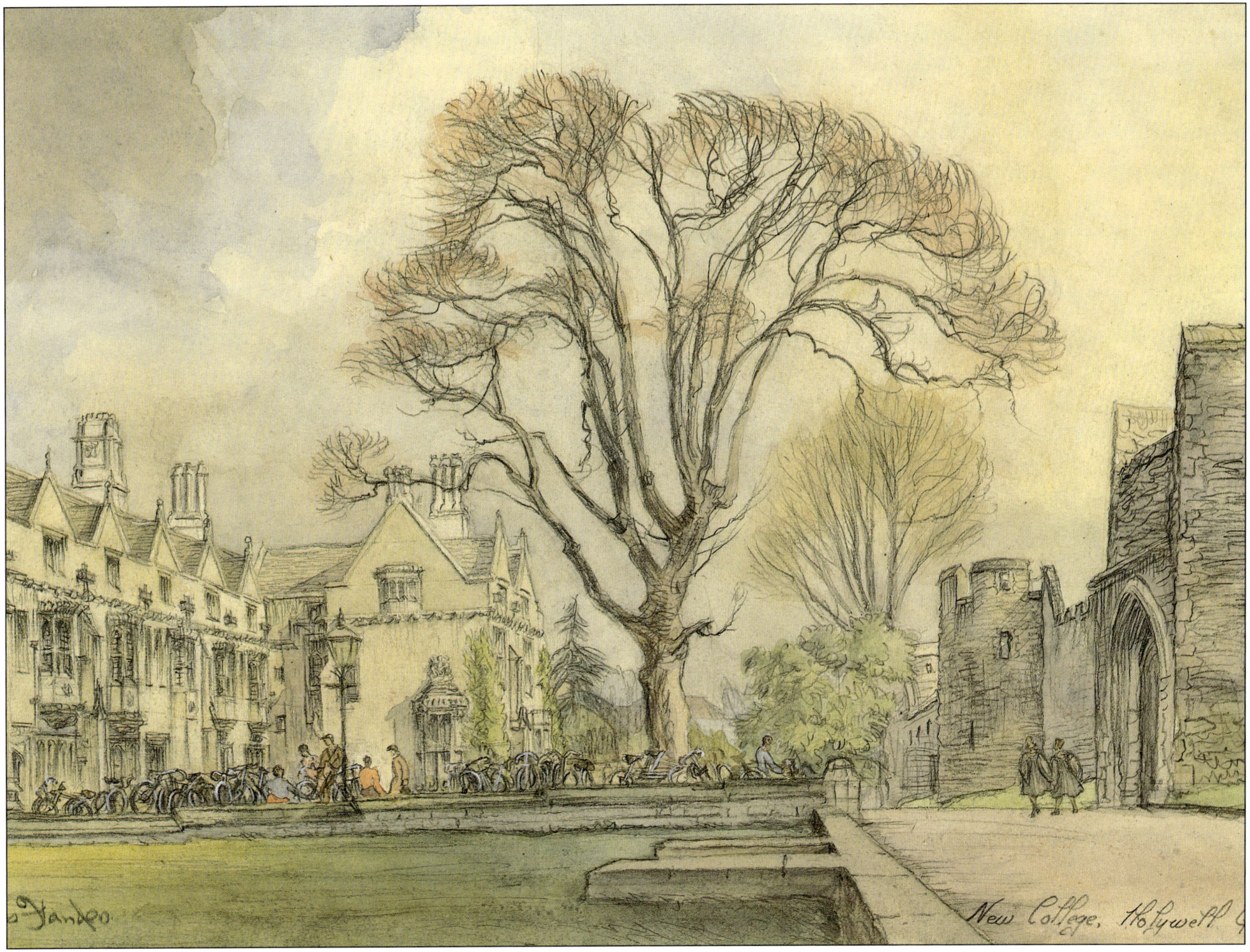
New College, Holywell

NUFFIELD COLLEGE

Dennis Flanders

Upper Quad

Viscount Nuffield, William Morris, was the first British manufacturer to develop the mass production of cheap cars, at Cowley, just outside Oxford. He was equally famous as a philanthropist and by the time he died in 1963, aged 85, he had given away £27 million.

In 1937, Lord Nuffield gave the University some land and £900,000 for the erection of a new college on the site of the basin of the Oxford Canal in New Road, opposite the Castle mound.

Austin Harrision's original design was modified at the wish of the founder and the war intervened before building could begin. The foundation stone was not laid until 1949 and the quadrangles were not completed until 1958, when the college received its Royal Charter. The College includes a small chapel designed by John Piper.

The tower, the first in Oxford for more than two hundred years, houses an open-access book stack. The tower is a hundred feet high and the flèche adds another sixty feet.

In this striking painting, Dennis contrasts to good effect the honey-coloured Clipsham (Rutland) stone of the buildings with the tower and copper-covered spire. It makes a neat and tidily attractive picture.

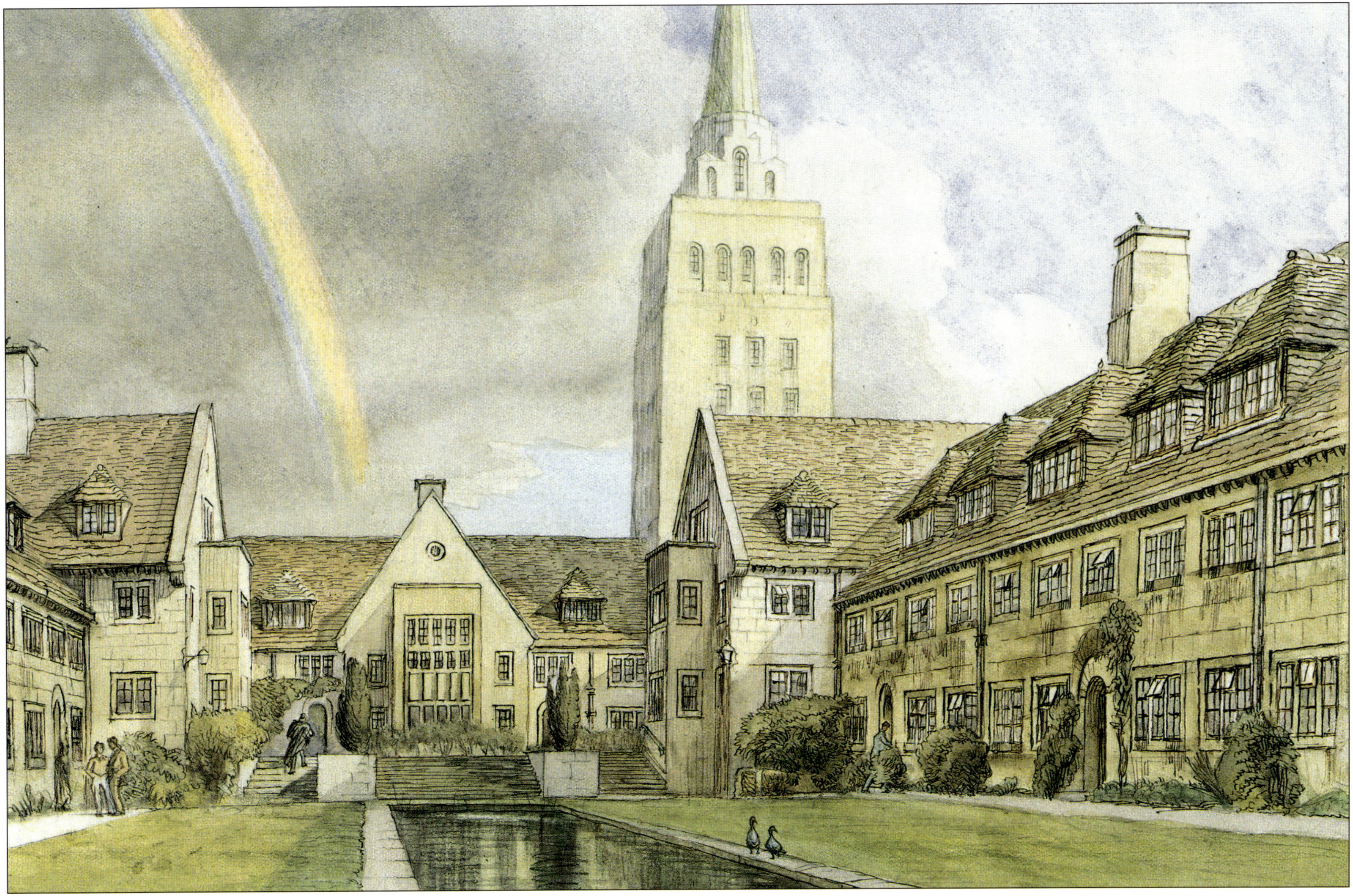

ORIEL COLLEGE

Ken Howard

Front Quadrangle

Founded by licence from King Edward II in 1326, Oriel can justly claim to be the first college to boast a royal founder.

In 1329 a large house, La Oriole, was gifted to the fledgling college by royal grant. This stood on the site of the present Front Quadrangle and was so called because of its *oratoriolum* or projecting upper window.

The present front quadrangle, with its Hall and Chapel, was begun in 1619 and completed in 1642. It was one of the largest building projects to be realised in pre-Restoration Oxford, was the largest in Oriel's history and yet, inexplicably, the architect is unknown.

In Ken Howard's painting, the Hall can be viewed immediately in front, through the arch of the entrance gateway from Oriel Square. It is approached up a small flight of steps under an open portico. Above the portico can be seen the words *Regnante Carolo*, referring to Charles I, during whose reign the Hall was built. During the Civil War, Charles I used Oxford as his campaign headquarters until his surrender in 1646. He used Oriel for meetings of the Privy Council.

In painting, effective compositions can come about through unexpected changes in the weather. Ken Howard was driven by persistent rainfall to shelter in the entrance gateway and he was struck by the pleasing effect of reflections in the puddles across the Front Quad. Ken commented that the combination of light, water and reflections is the reason painters never tire of Venice.

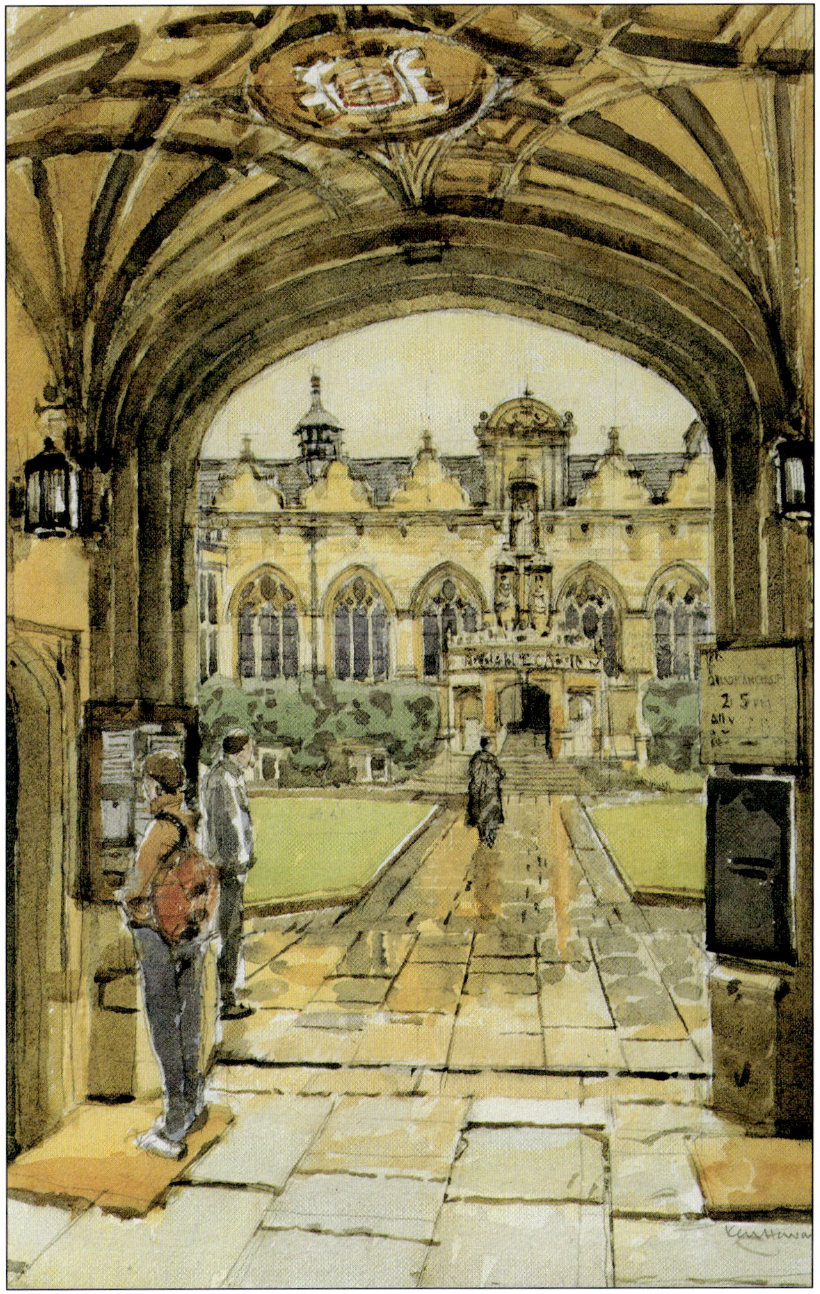

ORIEL COLLEGE

Ken Howard

Rhodes Building

Erected along the High Street in 1908 by Basil Champneys, the Rhodes Building commemorates one of Oxford's most influential graduates and patrons, Cecil Rhodes (1853-1902). It took him eight years to obtain his degree at Oriel due to the fact that not long after coming up in 1874 he was diagnosed as being terminally ill, so much so that he returned to South Africa where he had spent a short period prior to going up.

His health improved significantly and he returned to Oxford where, at the age of twenty-eight, he obtained his degree. Having made a huge fortune in Southern Africa, where Rhodesia was named after him, he was able to found the Rhodes Scholarships and leave £100,000 to Oriel College.

The Rhodes Scholarships were awarded to Americans, Germans and men from the colonies to further peace and understanding throughout the world.

Academic achievement was not to be the only criterion for the scholarships, a love of sports and leadership potential were also to be rewarded. Recipients include former American President Bill Clinton, Dom Mintoff, former Prime Minister of Malta, Norman Manley, former Prime Minister of Jamaica, James Fulbright, founder of the Fulbright Scholarships, and the American writer Edward de Bono.

In the period 1833-1845 three Oriel Fellows – John Keble, John Henry Newman and Edward Bouverie Pusey – were instrumental in founding the Oxford Movement. They were leading proponents of a return by the Anglican communion to more Catholic values.

Ken Howard's painting shows a busy High with the statue of Cecil Rhodes looking proudly from the first floor of the Rhodes Building. Next door, on the left, is the Old Bank which traces its origins back to 1771. It was taken over by Barclays in 1900. Recently it was closed and re-opened as the Old Bank Hotel.

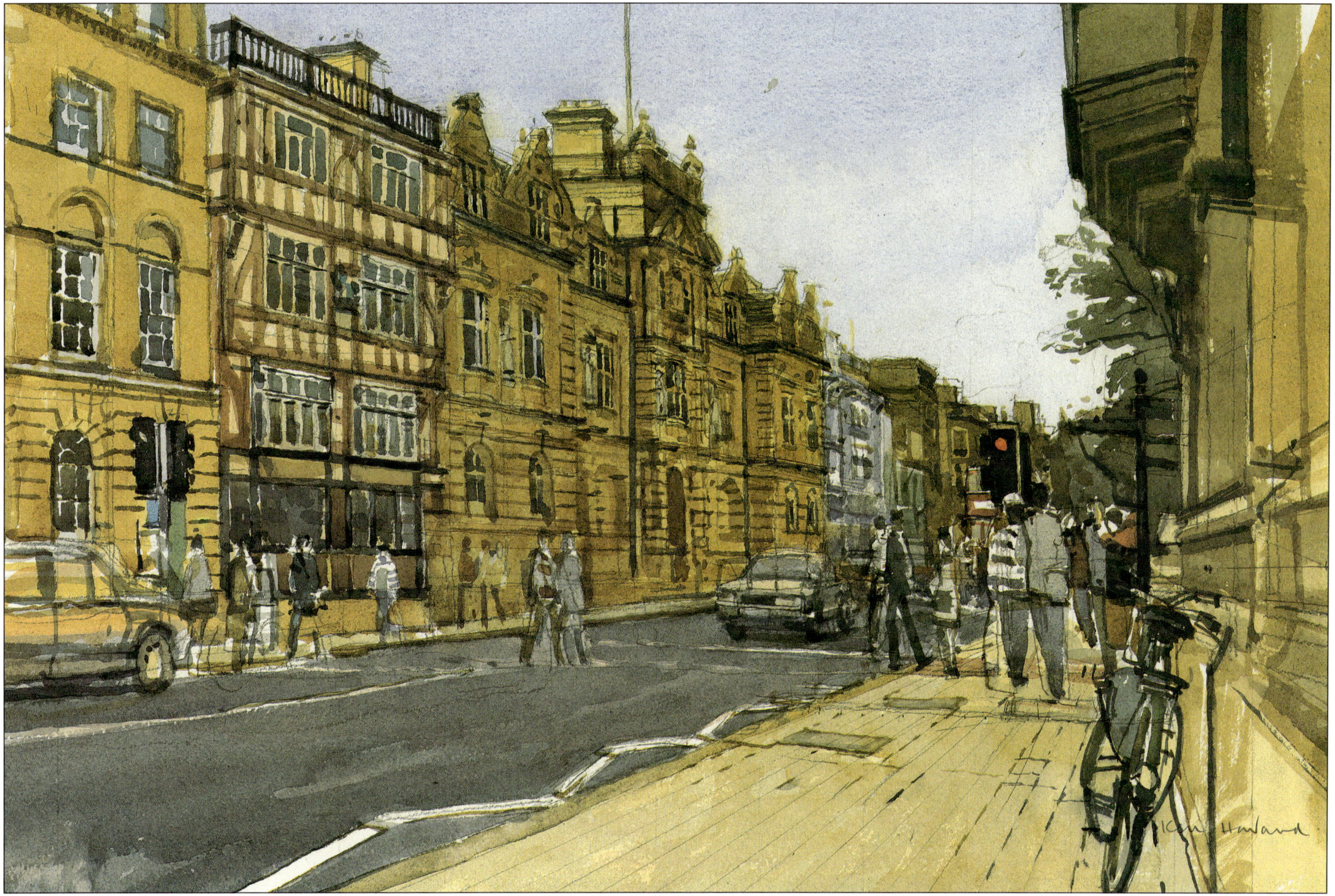

PEMBROKE COLLEGE

Dennis Roxby Bott

Pembroke Square

James I, a much underrated monarch in terms of encouragement of the arts and learning, was delighted when an opportunity occurred to found an Oxford college in 1624.

Named after the Chancellor of the University at that time, William Herbert, Third Earl of Pembroke, the college was endowed by two men from Abingdon, Thomas Teesdale and Richard Wightwick. Their endowment was originally meant for Balliol in return for securing places at that College for students from Abingdon School. Balliol was not happy with this arrangement and the benefactors and the Mayor and Corporation of Abingdon saw their opportunity to found a new college.

James I, always interested in academic matters, needed no persuasion and saw a great opportunity to further his credentials in this area – he immediately granted Letters Patent. The college maintains a connection with Abingdon School to this day.

Until the college built its own chapel in 1732, students worshipped in St Aldates Church across Pembroke Square. The boundary wall of the church can be seen to the left in Dennis Roxby Bott's tranquil painting of Pembroke Square and the Gate-tower entrance to the college.

When working on the painting Dennis used to arrive at about 5.30 on summer mornings as this was the only time of the day when the sun shone on the Gate-tower.

It also meant that he had two completely undisturbed hours, which was a strange feeling in a normally busy city such as Oxford.

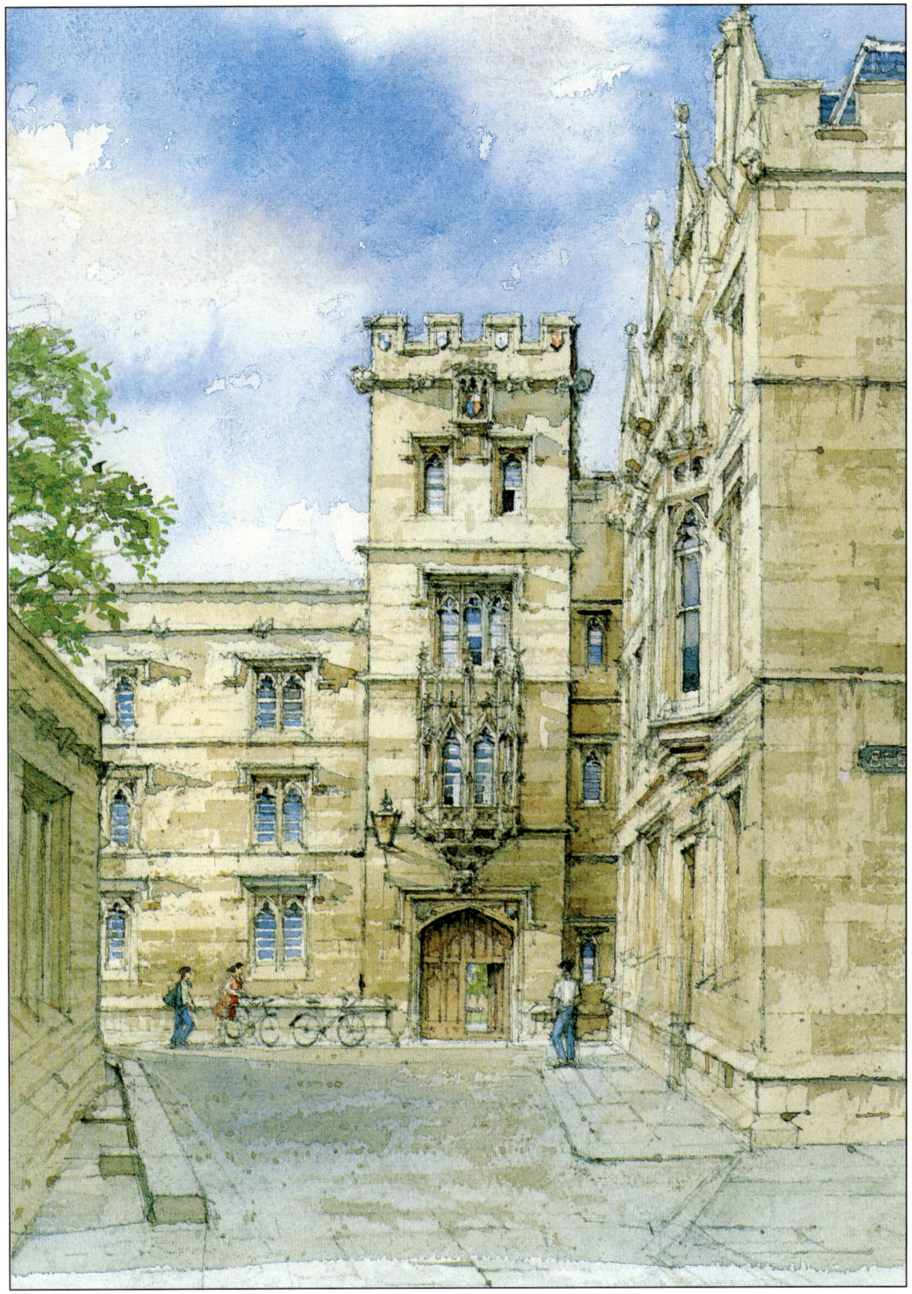

PEMBROKE COLLEGE

Dennis Roxby Bott

The Hall and Chapel Quad

Chapel Quad contains not only the chapel but also the Hall, which can be seen immediately facing through the arch in Dennis Roxby Bott's painting.

When the Hall was built in 1848 to a design by John Hayward it was the second largest in Oxford, and far too large for the needs of the limited student population. It was in the nature of an ego trip of the then Master, Francis Jeune, a great educational reformer in his day. It took the college many years to recover financially from his extravagance.

Another famous alumnus was Samuel Johnson who was at the college for just a year in 1728. He rebelled against its oppressive regime and left without taking a degree.

Even so, he held his college in great affection, returning many times, and in 1775 received an Honorary Doctorate from the University.

A wonderful climax to Dennis's commission to paint three pictures of Pembroke was an invitation to display his finished work at the annual garden party held at the end of Trinity Term in June, 1999. It was the climax of the famous Eights week – the occasion of the college bumping races, the purpose of which is to overtake and touch the boat ahead. Towards the end of a glorious summer afternoon guests left the garden party to cheer on the college crews, only to be totally soaked in one of the most violent thunderstorms of the summer.

Pembroke Men's Ist VIII, Head of the River in 1995, narrowly missed out on winning in 1999. In 2000 the 1st Women's VIII became Head of the River.

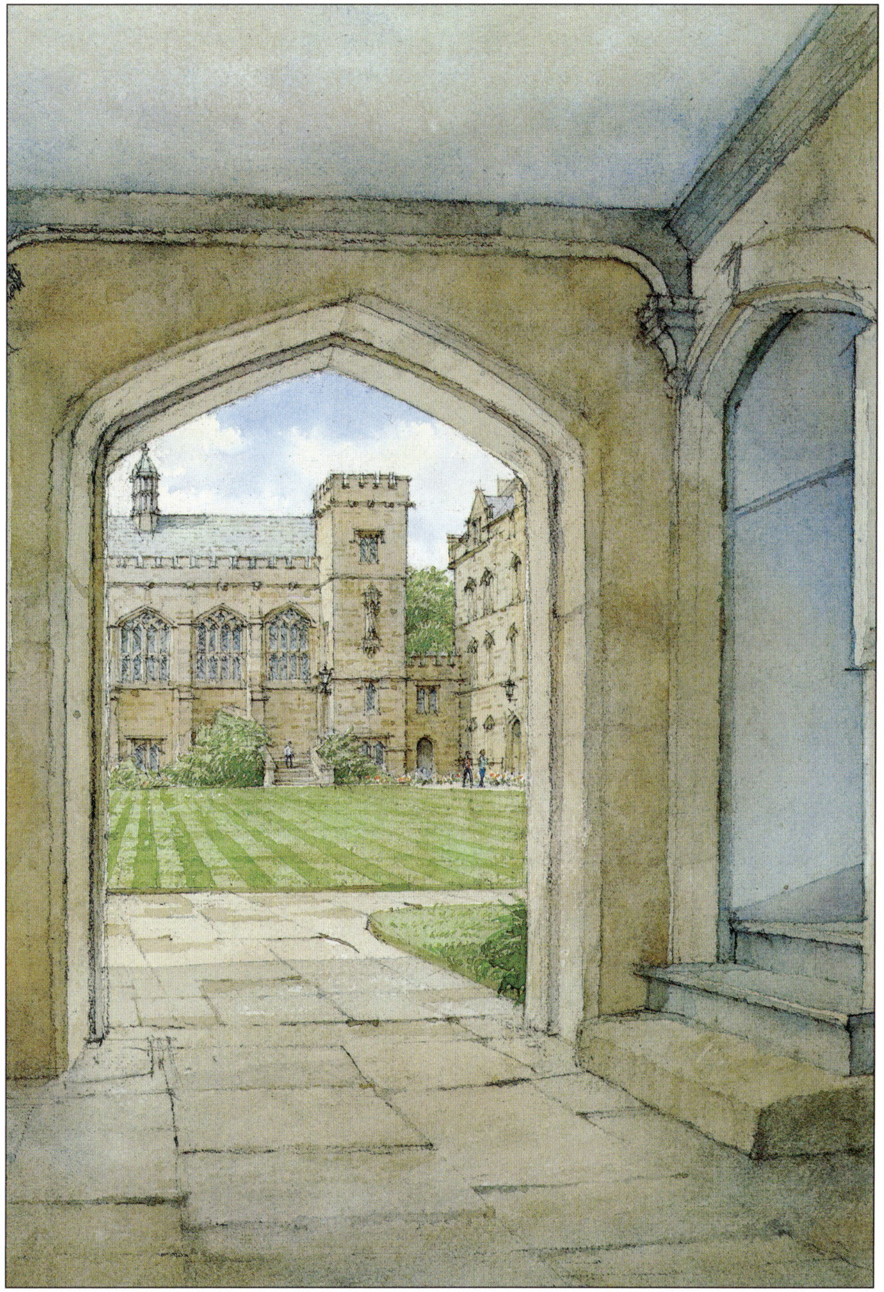

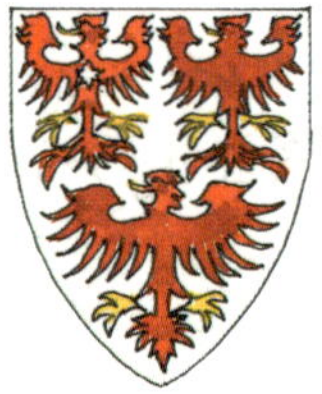

QUEEN'S COLLEGE

John Doyle

View from the High

Like some other mediaeval colleges, notably Exeter, Queen's had its statutes drawn up in such a way as to restrict entry to the geographical region of its founder.

Roger Eglesfield was a native of Cumberland and Chaplain to Queen Philippa – she who famously saved the defeated burghers of Calais from execution – wife of Edward III. Eglesfield used his position of influence with Philippa to gain livings and estates from Edward III and other influential friends. This provided a substantial endowment for his new college which was founded in 1341.

It is now more properly called The Queen's College because successive royal consorts have been patrons, particularly the wives of Charles I, George II and George III, who proved to be very generous benefactors. The present patron is Queen Elizabeth the Queen Mother.

For more than 500 years Cumberland and Westmoreland had a virtual monopoly on entry to Queen's. This was changed, however, like much else in Oxford, by the University Reform Act of 1854, whose leading architect was William Ewart Gladstone. The narrow parochialism which colleges encouraged was loosened with the setting up of the Hebdomadal Council, a centralized body, to run the University.

The classical architecture for which Queen's is famed is beautifully captured in John Doyle's painting, particularly the entrance screen and cupola which is thought to be based on the Luxembourg Palace in Paris. Under the cupola stands a six-foot statue of one of the patron queens, Caroline, wife of George III.

Incidentally, this and other classic views down the High would not be possible if it were not for a modern intruder into street architecture, the road bollard – so useful for artists to prop themselves up against in the middle of a busy road.

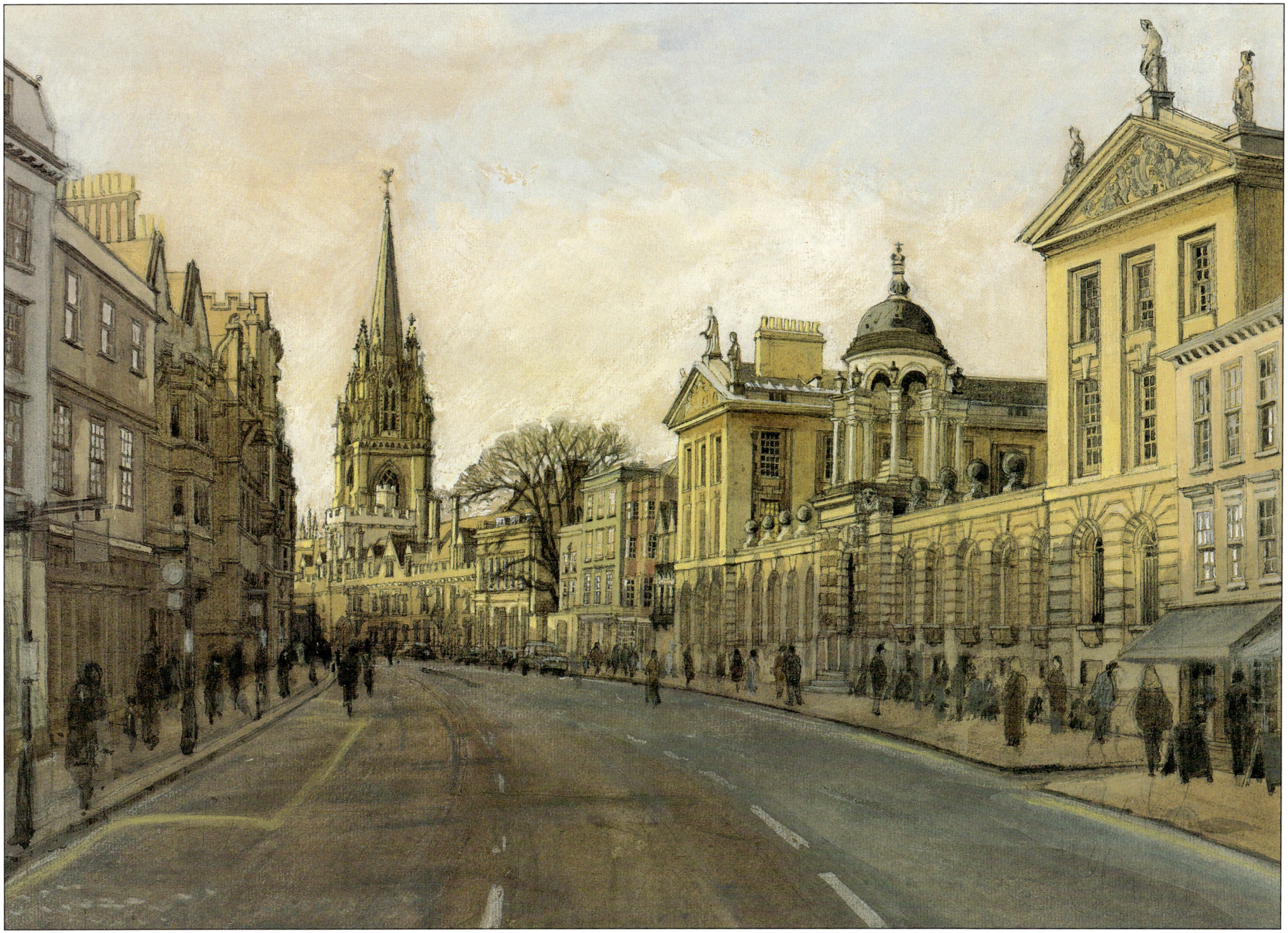

QUEEN'S COLLEGE

John Doyle

The Library

The building which houses this magnificent library, depicted in John Doyle's picture, was constructed by John Townesend between 1692-1696. The designer is not known but it is thought that Timothy Halton (Provost 1677-1704) may have been his own designer, with a little help from either Hawksmoor or Wren, who were around at the time. The stupendous plasterwork was crafted by James Hands, with rococo work by Thomas Roberts, and woodwork by Thomas Minns.

In John Doyle's painting, a statue of the first patron, Queen Philippa of Hainault, can be seen at the end of the library.

The Library building proved to be the catalyst for the complete rebuilding of Queen's, which was carried out by Halton's successor, Provost William Lancaster.

The Front Quadrangle was built by William Townesend (son of John) between 1709 and 1719, and according to Pevsner was the grandest piece of classical architecture in Oxford.

William Townesend's crowning glory, however, was the High Street front of 1734 with its wonderful entrance screen and cupola. Again it is thought that Nicholas Hawksmoor may have had some influence on the design.

The contribution of the Townesend family to major building works in Oxford during the 18th century was prodigious, being carried on by four successive generations. It included major works at eleven colleges, as well as the Radcliffe Camera, Magdalen Bridge, the Clarendon Buildings and many others.

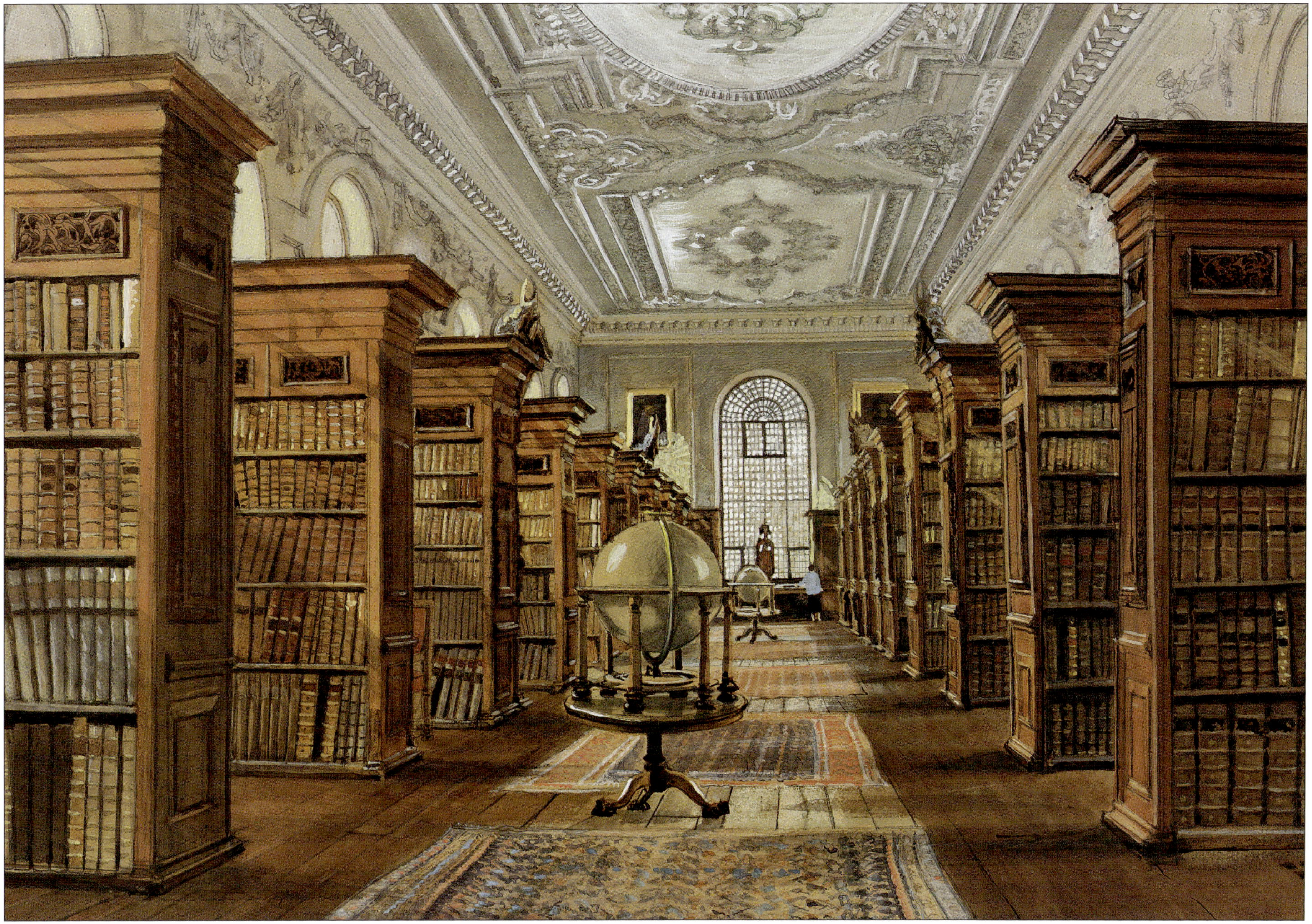

ST ANNE'S COLLEGE

Jane Carpanini

Hartland House

Unlike Lady Margaret Hall and Somerville, also founded in 1879, St Anne's was not a hall of residence. It catered for students living at home or in lodgings.

Mrs Bertha Johnson presided over the arrangements for Home Students from 1883 until 1921, when she retired as Principal. With help and support from her husband, Arthur Johnson, a Fellow at All Souls, she built up the Home Students' Organization to such an extent that in 1920, two hundred and fifty students matriculated. Finance and administration, however, were somewhat chaotic, so much so that in 1921 a new governing body was set up directly under the control of the University. As a result the University began to make grants towards administrative expenses. Accommodation for teaching, however, was still a problem.

In 1932 Mrs A G Hartland bought from St John's College the freehold of a site between Banbury Road and Woodstock Road. In 1938 a central building was erected to a design by Sir Giles Gilbert Scott and appropriately named Hartland House. It contains a fine library and all rooms are panelled in Japanese oak.

In 1952 St Anne's was granted full college status, and in 1991 Mrs Ruth Deech was elected Principal after serving the College for more than 20 years as a Fellow and tutor in Law. She is Chairman of the Human Fertilization and Embryology Authority.

Jane Carpanini's portrayal of St Anne's brings out one of the essential characteristics of this college – its sense of freedom. With students milling around the main lawns in front of Hartland House, it is a very good example of educational *art deco*.

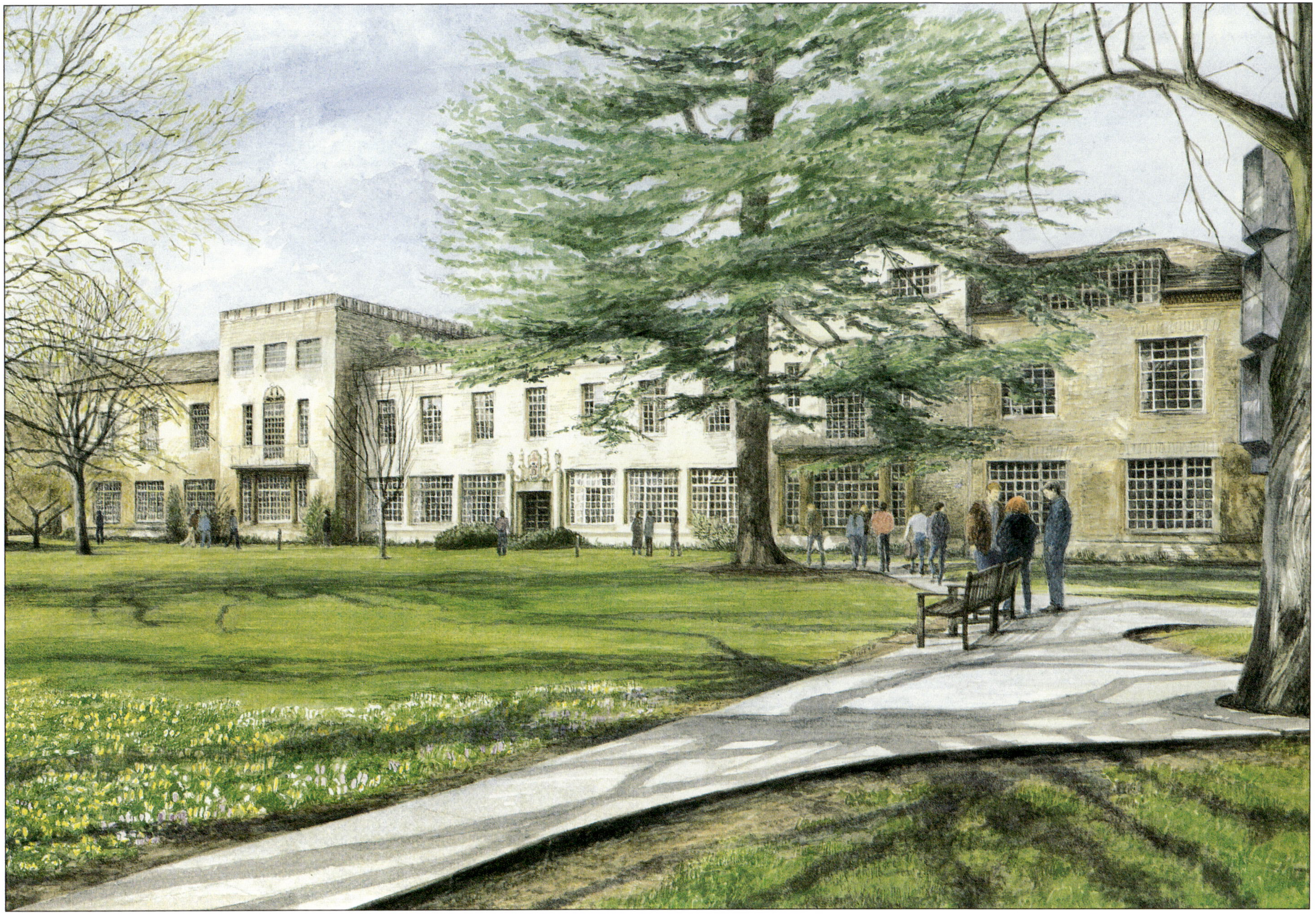

ST CATHERINE'S COLLEGE

Jane Carpanini

College Front

To enable people of limited means to obtain degrees, a non-collegiate Student Society was formed in 1868 – it became St Catherine's Society in 1930. It spared students the expense of college membership (board and lodging). The 1944 Education Act provided the means by which every undergraduate could afford residence in a college. As a result all those associated with St Catherine's were keen to see the Society become a fully integrated college.

The University Grants Commission offered St Catherine's £300,000 towards the cost of land and buildings. Much more was needed, and Alan Bullock (later Lord Bullock), the college's founding Master, undertook a vigorous fund-raising campaign, making successful appeals to the world of business and commerce.

The appointment of Arne Jacobs, a Danish architect, aroused controversy. He was asked to produce a totally integrated design for buildings, fittings and landscaped gardens. The strict geometry of the buildings is imaginatively softened throughout by the gardens which intersperse the college, with the yew hedges being a feature.

The college opened in October, 1962 and it is now the largest in Oxford. As there is no chapel, however, members use the nearby 13th century church of St Cross.

Due to its austere architecture, finding an artist willing and able to depict St Catherine's was not easy. Initially, the college wanted one of its distinguished artistic alumni to undertake the project. After much consideration he declined.

Jane Carpanini, however, found a solution to the problem by using a perspective which exploited Arne Jacobs's landscaped gardens to the full, diminishing the hard-edged profile of the buildings with the soft shapes of the trees and lawns, ably assisted by the Barbara Hepworth sculpture in the centre of the picture.

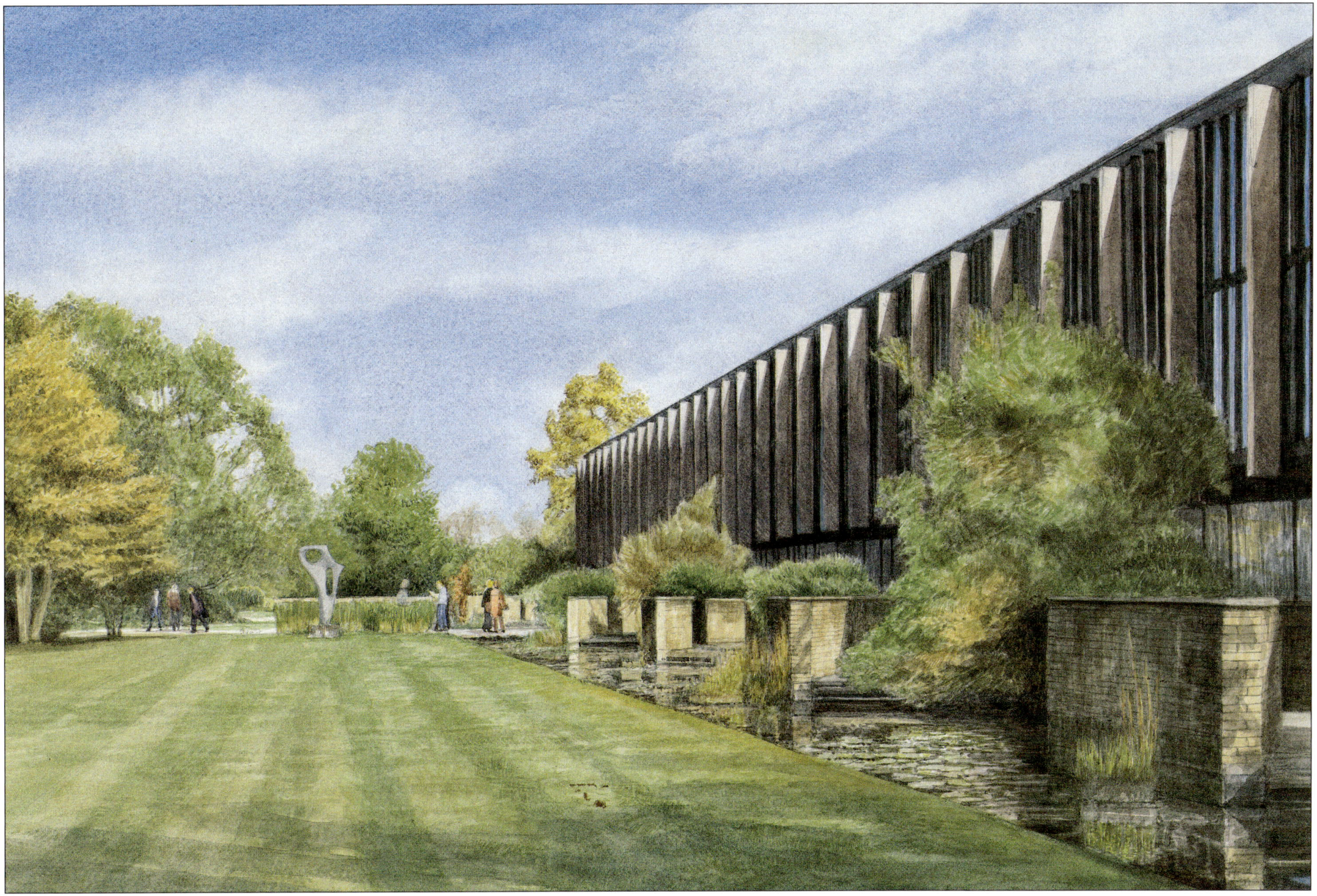

ST CROSS COLLEGE

Dennis Flanders

Pusey House

One of the University's younger graduate colleges, St Cross was founded in 1965.

It spent its first sixteen years in temporary accommodation on a site provided by Merton College just south of the mediaeval church of St Cross.

In 1981 the College moved to its present site in Pusey House on the west side of St Giles. The 999-year lease on the site excluded the chapel, and safeguarded the theological library and role of Pusey House in Oxford's pastoral life.

In 1989, the Master of St Cross, Dr Richard Repp, approached us about the possibility of commissioning a watercolour painting of the college to commemorate the 25th anniversary of its founding, and of producing limited edition prints.

He also mentioned that the college had a fine collection of 18th century watercolours, largely donated by Audrey Blackman, widow of Professor Geoffrey Blackman, the late Sibthorpian Professor of Rural Economy (1945-1970). The college is a veritable celebration of the gentle English art of watercolour painting, containing works by David Cox, Thomas Girtin, Peter De Wint, Paul Sandby and many others.

Dennis was thrilled at the prospect of his painting hanging alongside the very best of England's watercolourists. They were in good company.

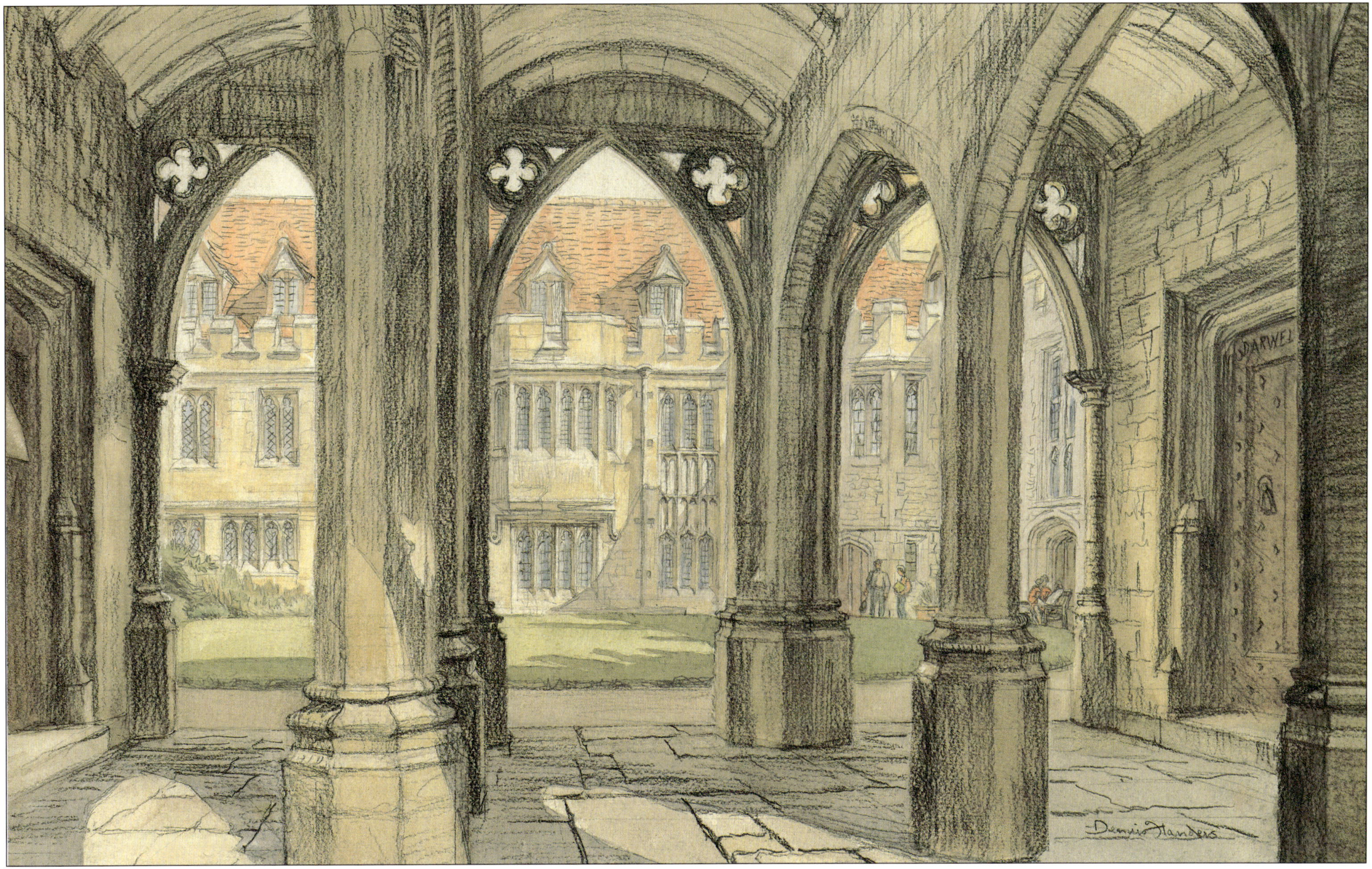
DARWEL
Dennis Flanders

ST EDMUND HALL

Ken Howard

Front Quadrangle

Going in an easterly direction along Oxford's High Street and just past Queen's College on the left is Queen's Lane. A little way down on the right-hand side is the entrance to St Edmund Hall. It is the sole survivor of the mediaeval Academic Halls in Oxford, which provided undergraduates with accommodation and tuition before the establishment of residential colleges as we know them today. It can claim to be the oldest academical society for the education of undergraduates in any university.

St Edmund's history goes back to the early 13th century, and it takes its name from St Edmund of Abingdon who taught in a house on the site of the present Front Quadrangle in the latter part of the 12th century. He later became Archbishop of Canterbury (1234-1240), but his embryo was not incorporated because it lacked the status and endowments which traditionally characterize colleges. In fact, until the dissolution it was owned by Osney Abbey. Queen's College acquired the freehold in 1557, and St Edmund Hall was very much under the aegis of Queen's until it finally gained its independence in 1957 when the Hall was granted its Charter of Incorporation as a college.

The painting Ken Howard has produced of this intimate little quadrangle illustrates perfectly his contention that you do not always want a sunny day. In certain instances a duller day is preferable because it emphasizes the subtle colours in the stonework. Bright sunshine can drown them in light. The diversity and richness of the colour in the stonework is a feature of Ken's lustrous watercolour.

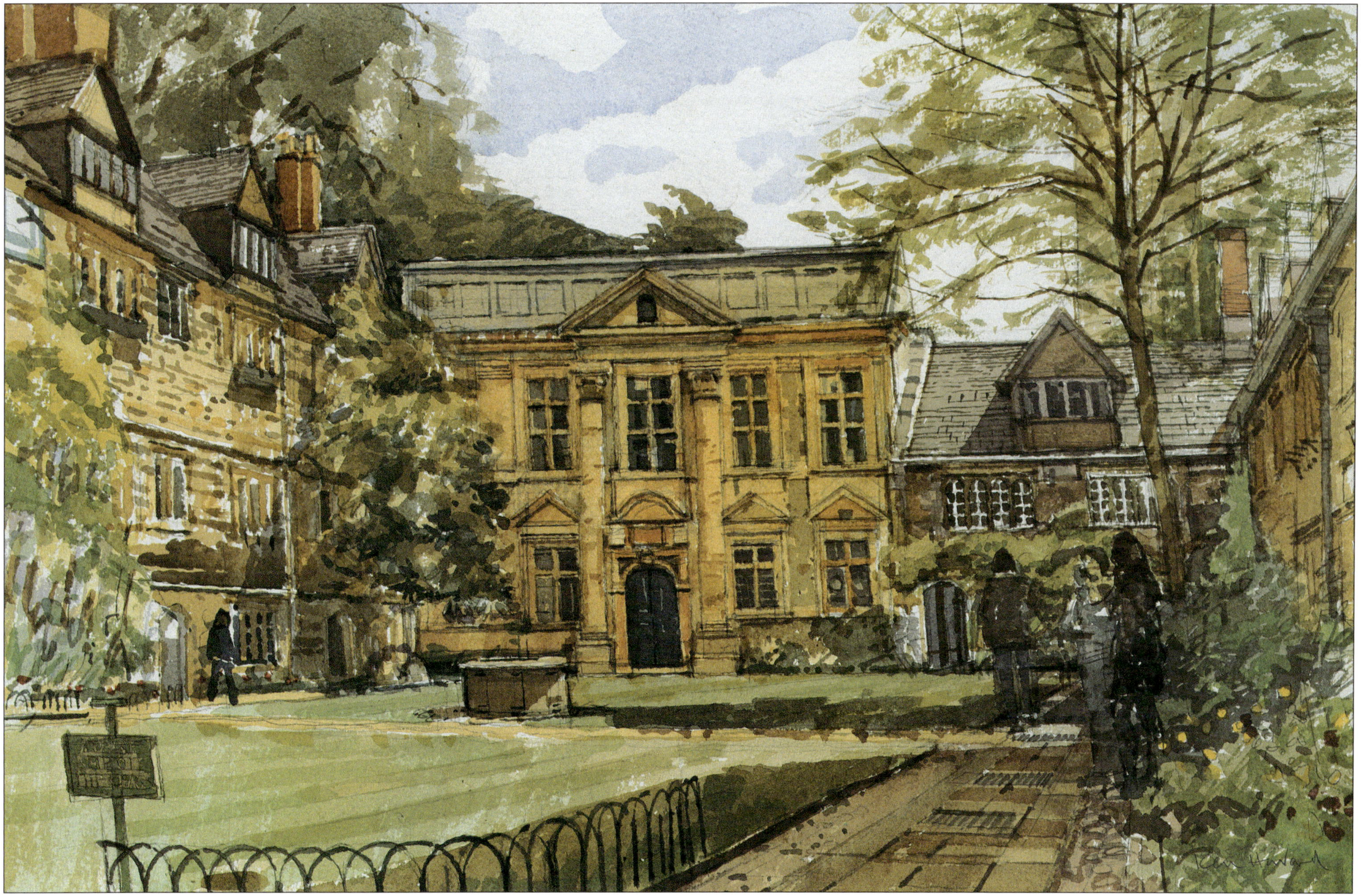

ST EDMUND HALL

Ken Howard

St Peter's in the East

The view of the College Front down Queen's Lane incorporates the redundant church of St Peters in the East, which has been converted into the college library. St Peter's dates from the 10th century, although the oldest surviving part is the 12th century crypt. The tower is 14th century, the entrance porch 15th century, and the church is described by Pevsner as "the most interesting in Oxford".

John Betjeman said it was like a village church set down unexpectedly in a town. Its living in mediaeval times was the wealthiest in Oxford. The restoration and conversion of the church into a library was carried out with great integrity to the original architecture. This was completed in 1970 with the tower becoming a book store.

St Edmund Hall is affectionately known as Teddy Hall, and long before they became generally available teddy bears were marketed by the college as souvenirs.

In Ken Howard's painting can be seen a great profusion of bicycles – an integral part of the Oxford scene. They have gained even greater prominence since the banning in 1999 of motor cars from Oxford City Centre during the day.

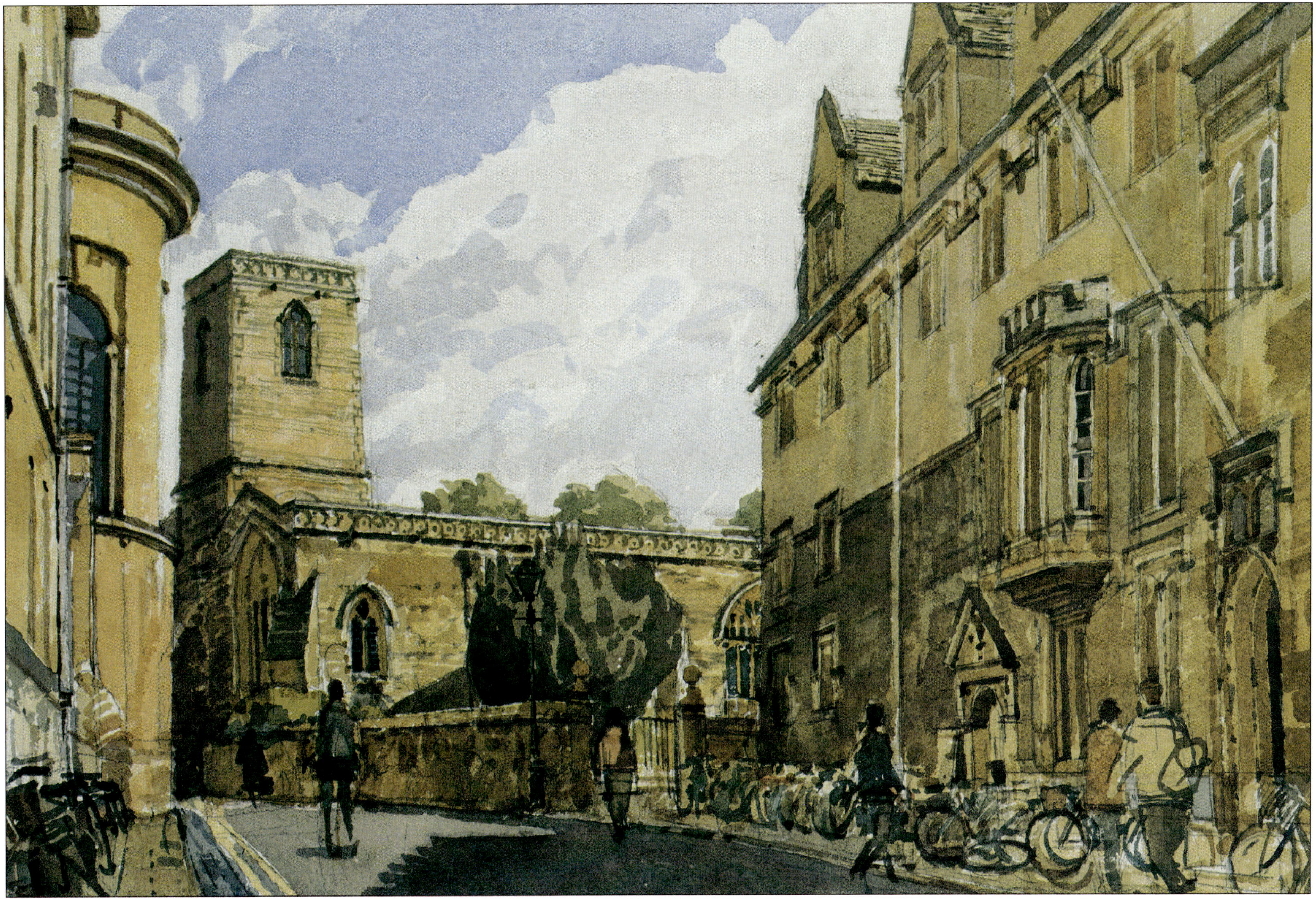

ST HILDA'S

Jane Carpanini

Milham Ford

St Hilda's was founded in 1893 by Miss Dorothea Beale, Principal of Cheltenham Ladies' College, whose aim was to provide a hall of residence where her pupils from Cheltenham could take advantage of the recent female emancipation of Oxford. Miss Beale purchased Cowley House in Cowley Place, which has a beautiful situation beside Milham Ford on the River Cherwell. She financed it for the first four years.

The college is named after St Hild, the 7th century founder and Abbess of Whitby, and a great educator of women. This seems wholly appropriate in the context of a woman's place in society in the late 19th century.

St Hild was the embodiment of Anglo Saxon women and their equal place with men in that society. The Normans changed all that, but Oxford's newly-founded female colleges started to redress the imbalance.

In the year 2001 St Hilda's remains the only exclusively-female college in Oxford.

Whilst making her drawing, Jane Carpanini bemoaned the fact that there were no punts on the Cherwell to complete the scene. Students from St Hilda's who were looking over her shoulder enthusiastically agreed to correct this omission. It was quite obvious that they had not undertaken this activity before. Jane, however, was grateful because it completed the scene and no-one was drowned.

Jane Carpanini's portrayal of Milham Ford is timeless; the epitome of an English riverside scene in summer.

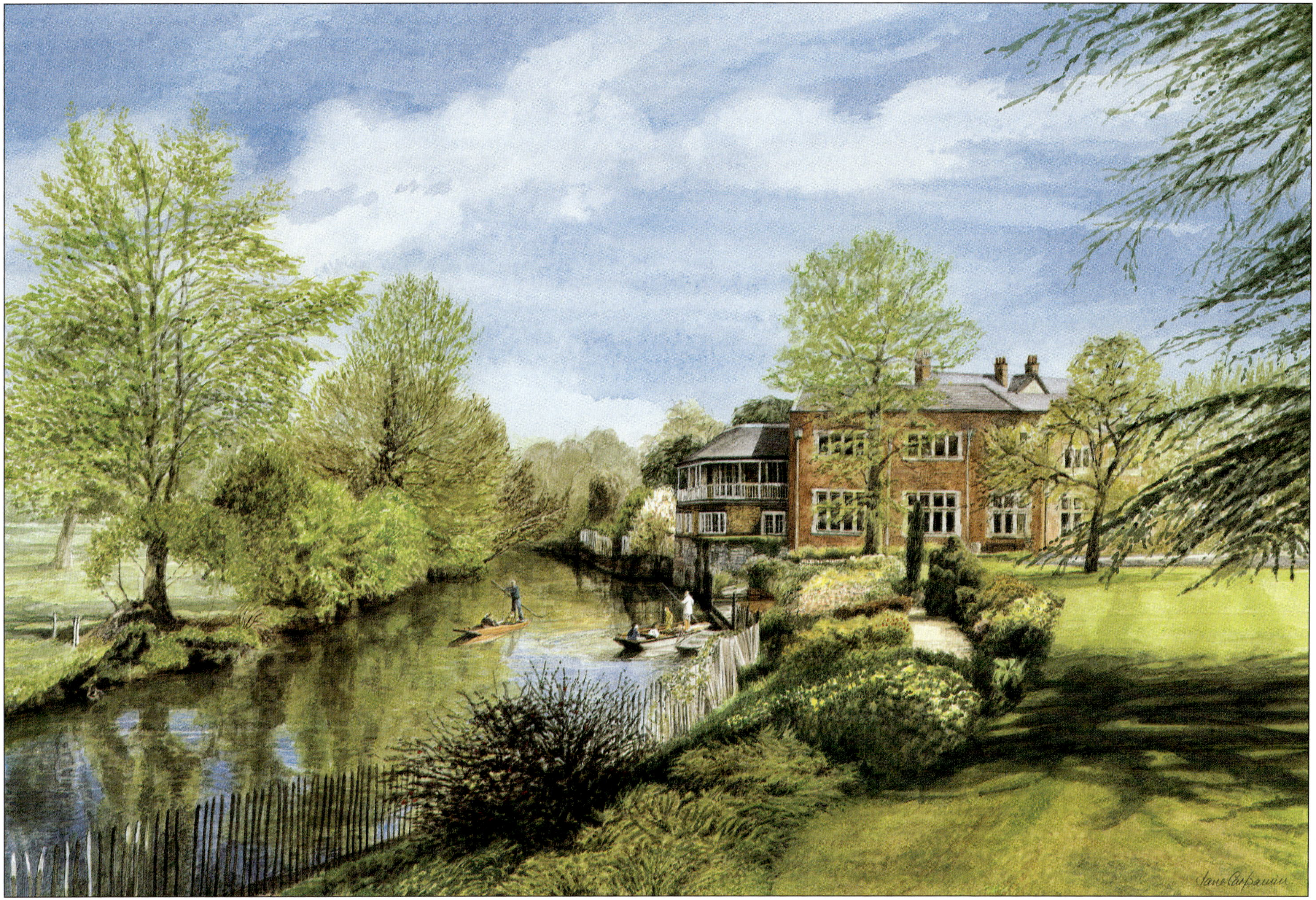

ST JOHN'S COLLEGE

John Doyle

Canterbury Quad

The classical lines of the Canterbury Quadrangle, with its arcaded loggias and the heavily decorated statues of Charles I and his wife Queen Henrietta, were based on the 15th century Foundlings Hospital in Florence. The Quad was built by St John's most famous alumnus, Archbishop Laud (1573-1645).

St John's was originally founded by Archbishop Chichele in 1437 as the St Bernard College for Cistercian students. It was dissolved in 1539 during the Reformation along with other monastic colleges.

In 1555 a wealthy Roman Catholic clothier, Sir Thomas White, purchased the St Bernard site and buildings to found St John's College. This was the second Oxford college to be founded that year in gratitude for the restoration of Catholicism under Mary I. Trinity was the other.

This lead to three prominent Protestants, Bishops Latimer, Ridley and Archbishop Cranmer, being burnt at the stake in Broad Street in 1555 and 1556. Their martyrs' memorial stands adjacent to St John's in St Giles, and was architect George Gilbert Scott's first work in Oxford.

When Mary was succeeded by her Protestant sister, Elizabeth, the tide turned and one of St John's first fellows, Edmund Campion, became Oxford's most celebrated Catholic martyr when in 1581 he was executed at Tyburn. Thence forward Roman Catholics were not officially allowed to attend the University again until 1895.

The college already had in its possession an evocative chalk drawing from 1936 by Sir Muirhead Bone, made from the south-west corner. John Doyle was keen to produce a watercolour painting looking from the north-west corner, which he felt would give the possibility of more sunlight.

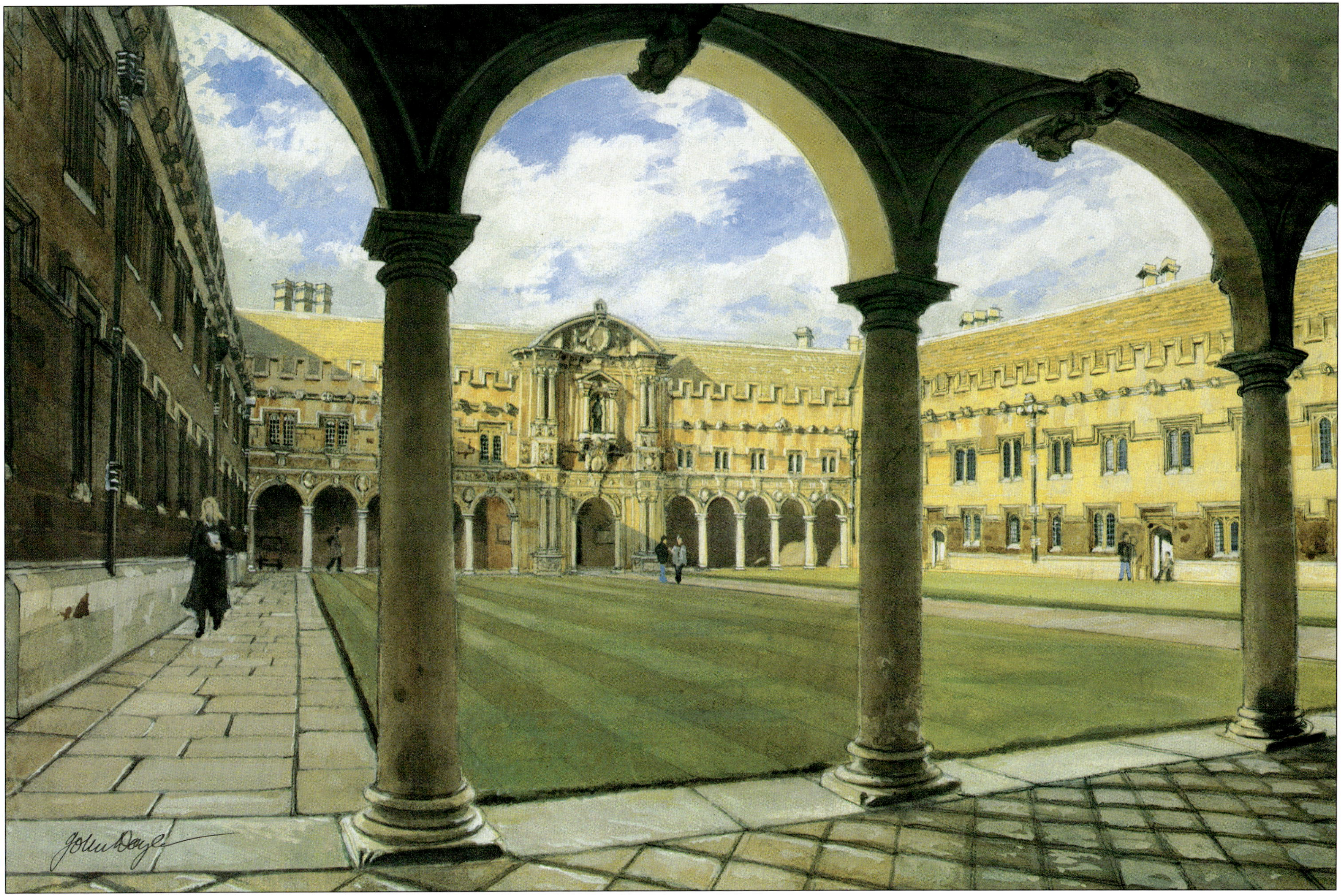

ST JOHN'S COLLEGE

John Doyle

Garden

Archbishop Laud was President of St John's from 1611-1621, Chancellor of the University from 1630 until 1641, and Archbishop of Canterbury from 1633. In addition, he was successfully Bishop of Rochester, St David's in Wales, Bath and Wells, and Bishop of London. He rationalized the University statutes into what became known as the Laudean Code which was accepted by the University convocation in 1636.

Laud enjoyed the regard and favour of Charles I and by 1633 had become virtually first minister of the Crown. Laud's overzealous attempt to enforce the doctrines of high church and Charles I's power over Parliament lead in 1640 to his impeachment by the Long Parliament. He was eventually found guilty of endeavouring to overthrow the Protestant religion and acting as an enemy to Parliament. He was beheaded on Tower Hill in 1645. Initially buried in All Hallows, his body was translated to St John's College in 1663.

John Doyle's very pretty view of St John's beautiful gardens has the Laud Library in the background. It is one of the most impressive gardens in Oxford, landscaped in part by Capability Brown in the 18th century, and greatly enhanced in the 20th century by Professor Geoffrey Blackman.

A notable alumnus of more recent times is British Prime Minister, Tony Blair, who was also married in the College Chapel.

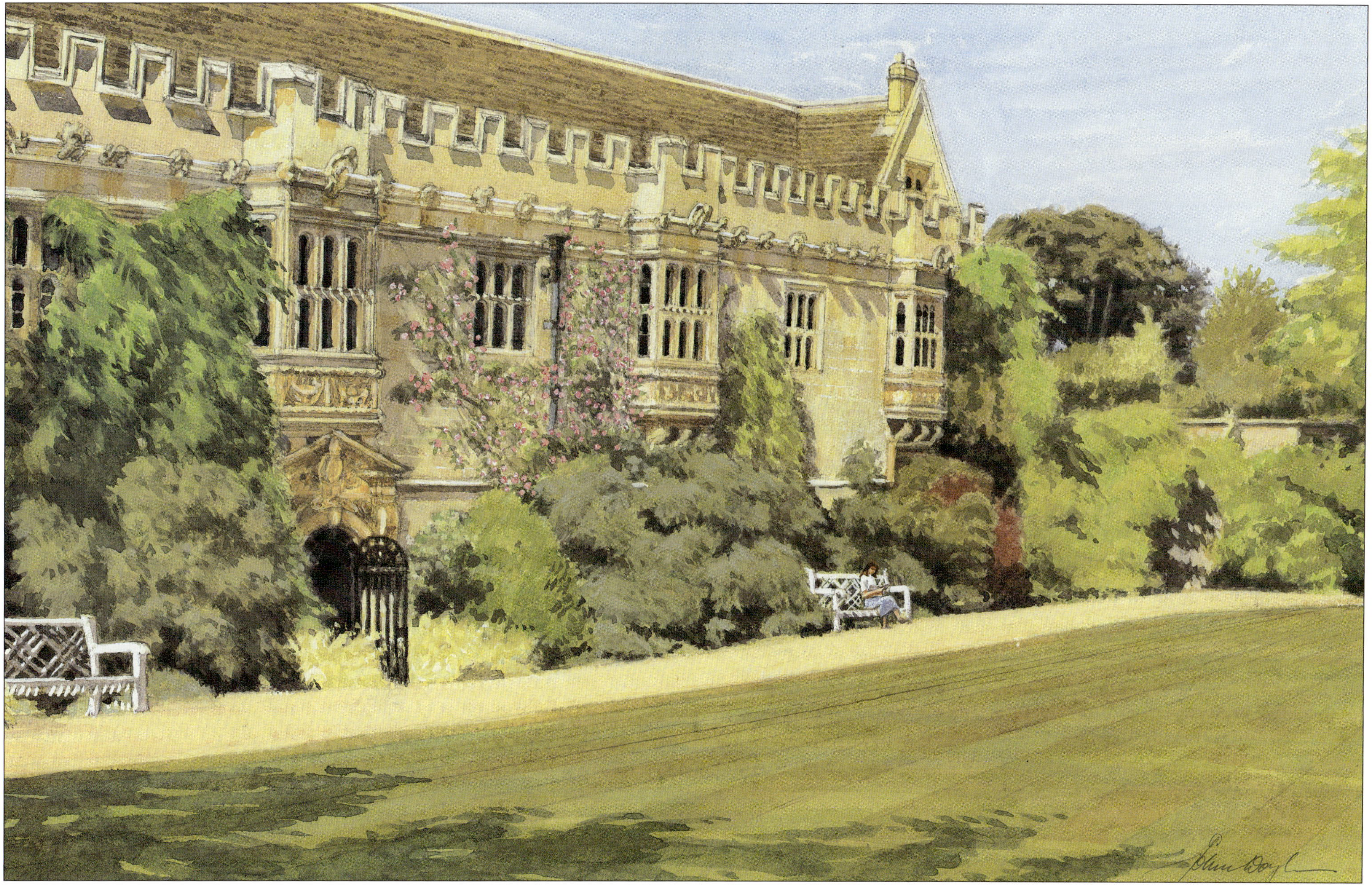

ST PETER'S COLLEGE

Jane Carpanini

Linton House

Founded in 1929 by the Bishop of Liverpool, Francis Chavasse, St Peter's occupies the site of Trillicks Inn (c1300), which was rebuilt in 1476 and renamed New Inn Hall.

The college's connection with the Church of St Peter-le-Bailey through the influence of successive Rectors, Henry Linton 1864-1879, and Francis Chavasse 1879-1899, the eventual founder of the college, is crucial. An earlier church had been demolished in 1874 as part of a road-widening scheme and a new one erected in New Inn Hall Street to a design by Basil Champneys.

In 1877, Rector Henry Linton bought a nearby Georgian House for use as the rectory for the parish. It had formerly been the headquarters of the Oxford Canal Company. It is now known as Linton House, part of which forms the Weldon Lodge entrance to Linton Quad.

The New Hall Inn buildings were acquired in 1929 by Christopher Chavasse, the son of the founder – his father died in 1928 – who was himself Rector of St Peter's from 1927-1939. He added the rectory to the stock of college buildings and became its first Master in 1929.

In 1935, when the church was closed due to parish amalgamation, it became the Chapel of St Peter's. This explains why it has a large Victorian parish church as its chapel, which is probably rather too large for normal college use, but nonetheless quite magnificent.

Lord Nuffield (William Morris) was a great benefactor who redeemed the college's mortgage in the 1930s, and provided the Emily Morris Building in memory of his mother.

Until the 1960s, successive Masters were also vicars of the parish and part of the college's crucial connection with St Peter-le-Bailey.

The present Master, classicist Dr John Barron, is immensely proud of a recent gift of stained glass from the family of the late Hungarian refugee artist, Ervin Bossanyi, which are the prototypes of his famous windows in Canterbury Cathedral.

Jane Carpanini felt that St Peter's was different from the traditional cloistered colleges, being more open and obviously part of the busy city centre scene. More town than gown.

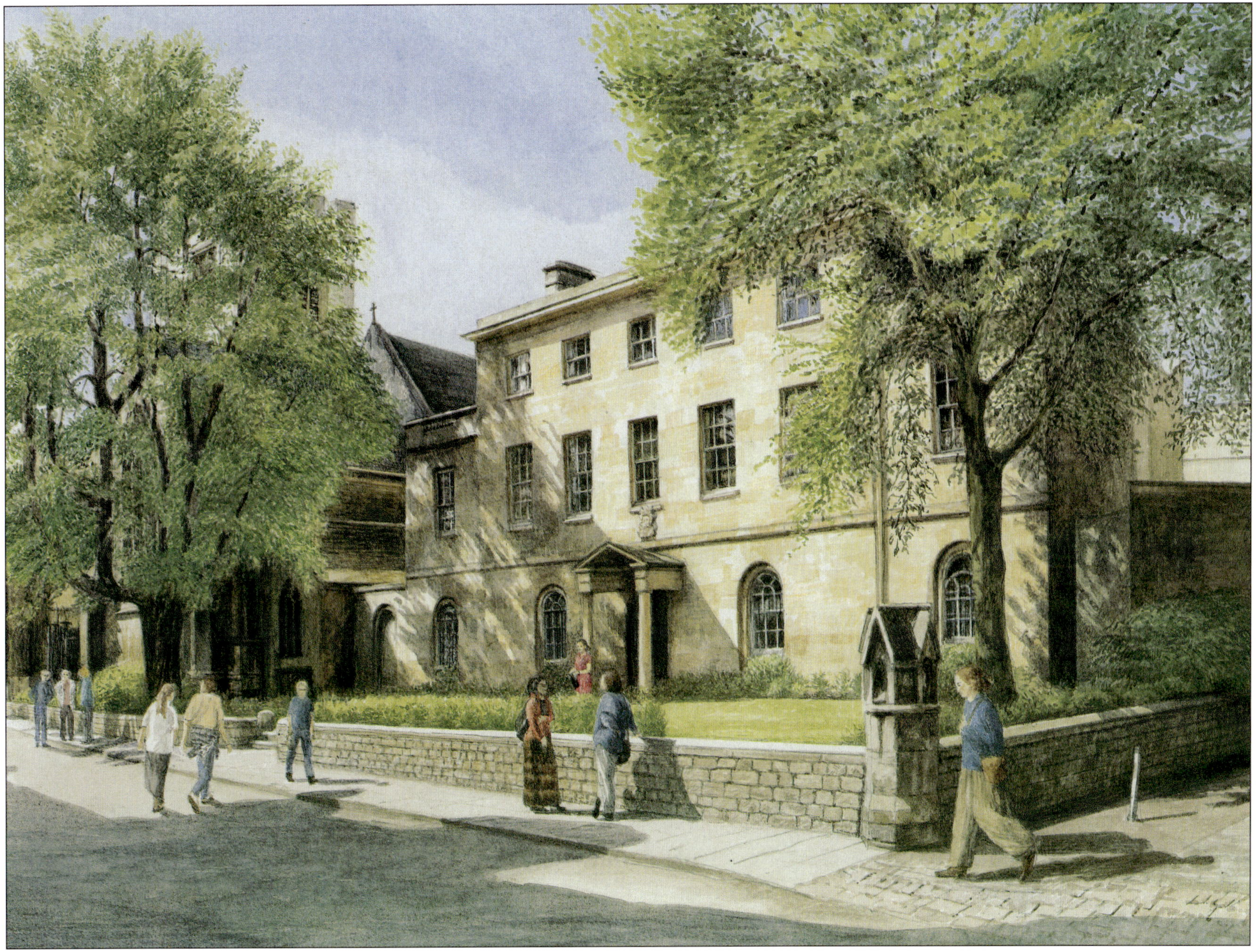

SOMERVILLE COLLEGE

Jane Carpanini

The Darbishire Quadrangle

The first Principal of Somerville was Miss Madelaine Shaw Lefevre (1879-1889). Sister of a Liberal Member of Parliament and niece of a former Speaker of the House of Commons, she was adroit politically and managed to allay the apprehensions people felt towards the new female Halls.

She was clearly successful because such a conservative as John Ruskin was won over, and presented Somerville with books and pictures, and a gift of precious stones, the Ruskin Jewels, which were to form the basis of the Principal's regalia on formal occasions.

Through the traditional 1892 gatehouse entrance in Woodstock Road is the neat Darbishire Quad. It was designed by Morley Holder with pleasant stone buildings of 17th century style, and completed in 1934. A year later Dorothy L Sayers, a distinguished alumnus of Somerville, published *Gaudy Night* – the most celebrated portrayal of life in a women's college. In 1996, Dame Fiona Caldicott became Principal. She is President of the Royal College of Psychiatrists.

Jane Carpanini's panoramic view of the small Darbishire Quad illustrates perfectly the importance of the optical laws governing perspective, and the advantage a talented and experienced artist has over a photographer.

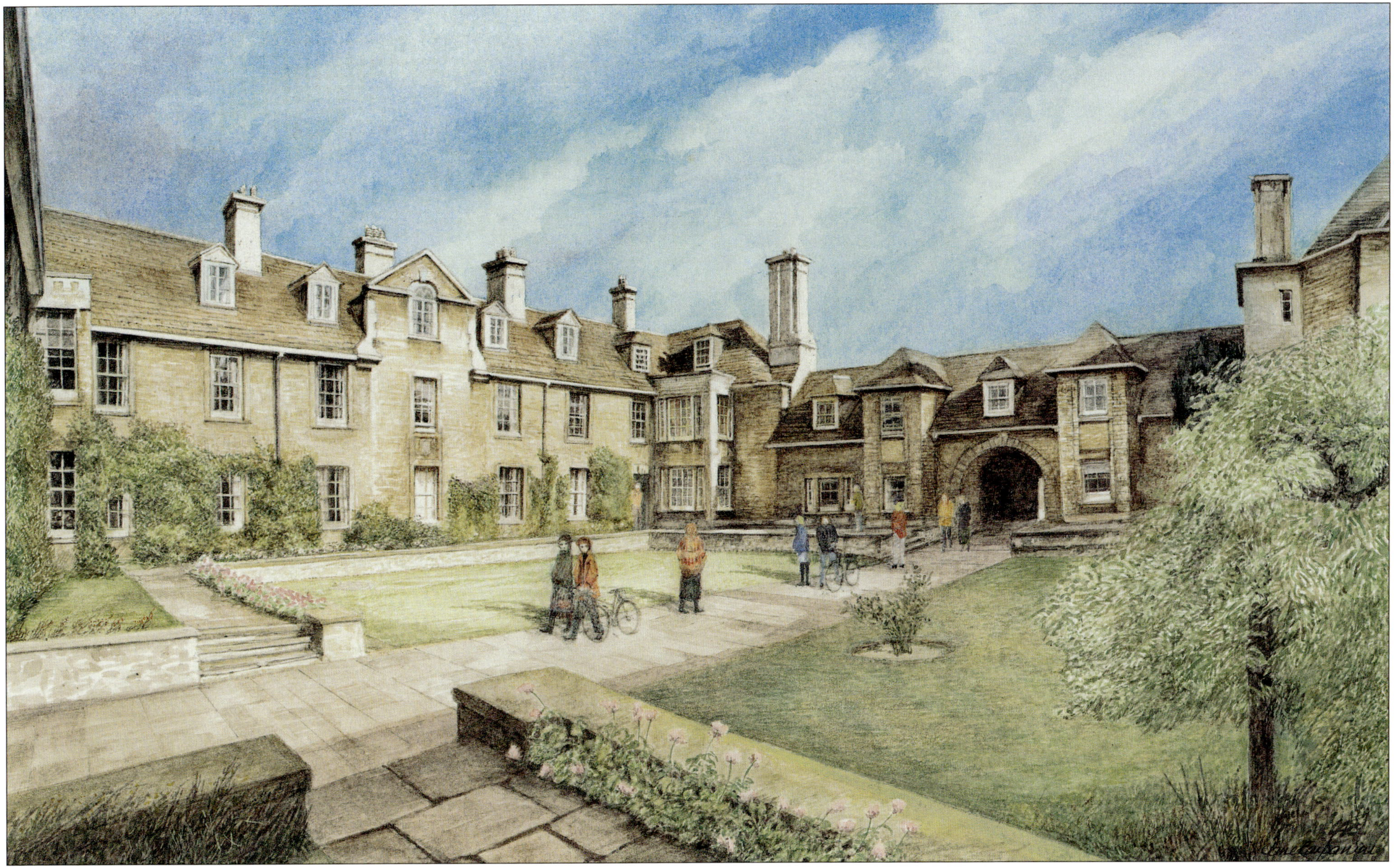

SOMERVILLE COLLEGE

Dennis Flanders

The Garden Quad

Somerville was the second ladies college to be founded in Oxford but unlike the first, Lady Margaret Hall, it is non-denominational. In 1994 it gave up its female-only status thus leaving St Hilda's as the only exclusively female college in Oxford. It was named in honour of Mary Somerville (1780-1872), an eminent mathematician.

Since the last war Somerville has produced two lady Prime Ministers, Indira Ghandi (India, 1966) and Lady Margaret Thatcher (Great Britain, 1979). Other distinguished female scholars include Dorothy L Sayers, Iris Murdoch, Shirley Williams, and the Nobel Prize winner, Dorothy Hodgkin.

One morning in the spring of 1988, I heard the Principal of the College, Daphne Park, being interviewed on Radio 4 about her fund-raising trip to America.

I later telephoned her to see whether we could channel her fund-raising zeal towards the production of limited edition prints of Somerville. Once she realized that financially there was no risk for the College, she readily agreed.

Daphne Park had spent much of her working life in the service of government in the diplomatic and intelligence field. Her physical appearance – a small, well-rounded Miss Marple with a kindly demeanour – seemed to contradict her former profession. That was partly the reason, I'm sure, she was so successful in her diplomatic career.

Dennis painted a wonderfully evocative picture across the lawns (ignoring the seasonally erected tennis nets) to capture the familiar lines of the Library, and the House and Hall. The Pfeifer Library, on the left in Dennis's painting, was designed by Basil Champneys and completed in 1903.

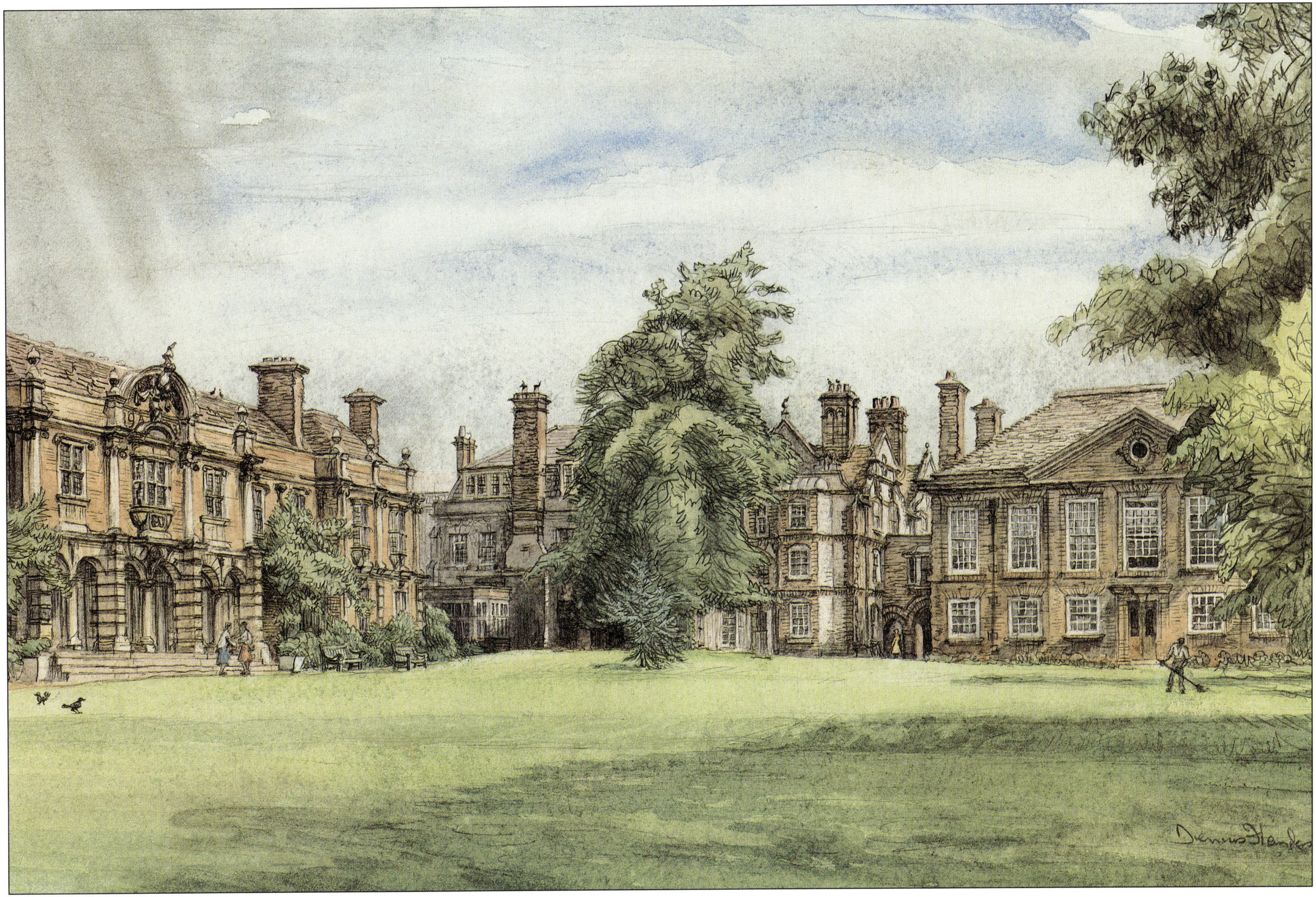

TRINITY COLLEGE

John Doyle

Chapel and Front Quadrangle

The open and spacious Front Quadrangle, laid to lawn with mature trees around its perimeter, is quite different from any other. It can easily be viewed through the railings of the Broad Street Front.

Trinity was founded by Sir Thomas Pope in 1555 in gratitude for the restoration of Catholicism under Mary Tudor. He was clearly an adroit politician because he served her father, Henry VIII, and brother, Edward VI, as Treasurer of the Court of Augmentation. It was his job to gather together the estates of the monasteries dissolved at the Reformation. In the process he amassed for himself a considerable fortune, part of which he used to purchase the site and buildings of one of the dissolved monastic foundations, Durham College. This became Trinity College.

Durham College was founded in 1291 for the Benedictine monks of Durham Cathedral as a place of study in Oxford. The only surviving Durham College building is Trinity's Old Library, completed in 1494.

Sir Thomas Pope was also a guardian of Mary's sister, Princess Elizabeth, at Hatfield House, and she found his company most congenial.

He died in 1559, a year after Elizabeth came to the throne, so in effect he served four Tudor sovereigns. He is believed to be the only founder of an Oxbridge College to be buried under his own foundation.

John Doyle's painting shows the well-manicured foreground leading to Trinity's unusual Chapel. It was the first non-gothic chapel to be built in Oxford, when it replaced the earlier 13th century Durham College Chapel in 1694. Henry Aldridge, Dean of Christ Church, is thought to have been very influential in its design, with help and advice from Christopher Wren.

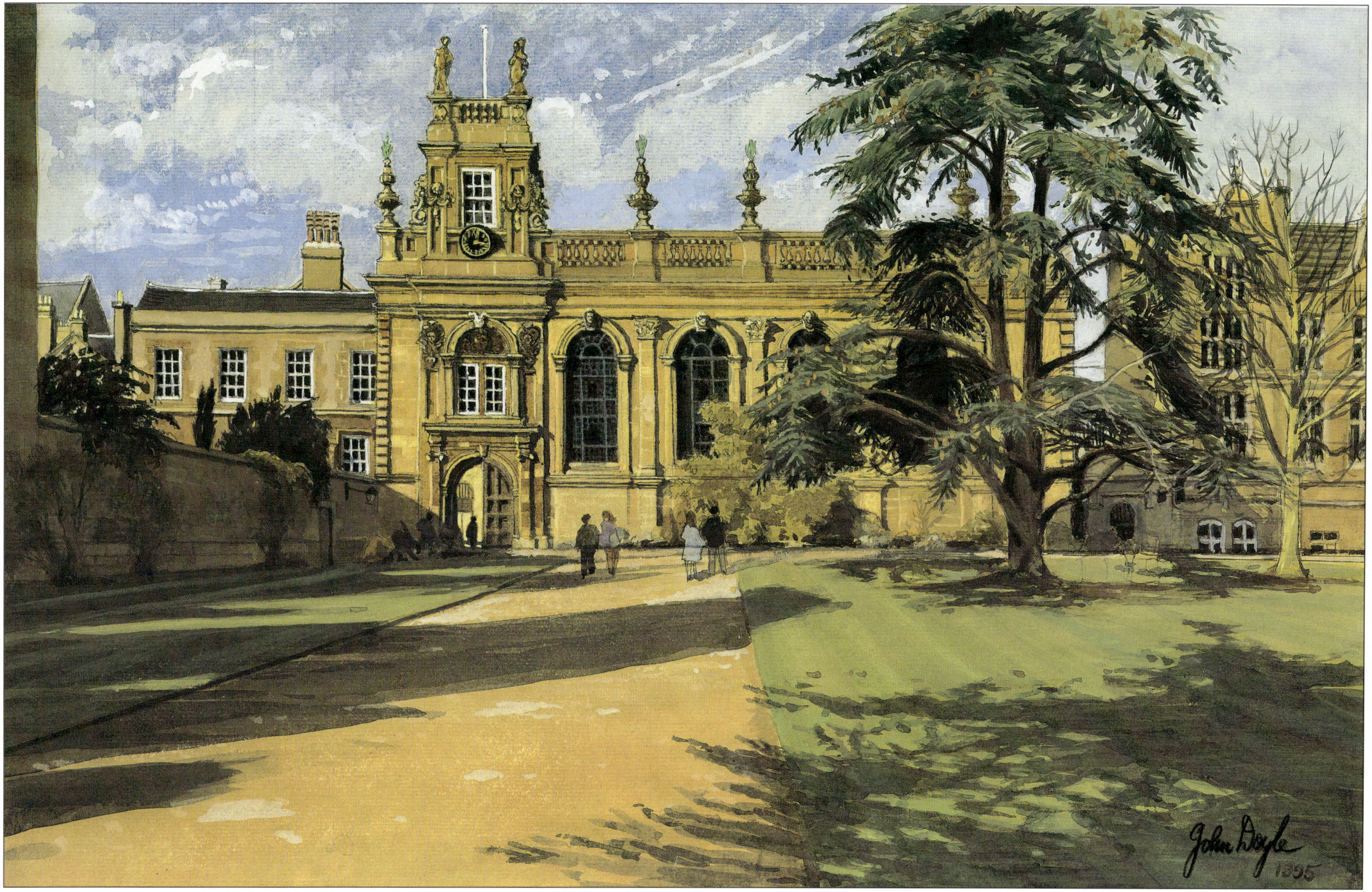
John Doyle
1995

TRINITY COLLEGE

John Doyle

The Garden Quadrangle

John Doyle's view of the Garden Quadrangle from Parks Road was painted in the late afternoon to catch the long shadows, which very effectively break up the vast expanse of lawn.

The spire of Balliol Chapel can clearly be seen to the right in John's painting. Immediately in front of this is the centre building of the Open Quadrangle, designed by Christopher Wren and erected in 1682. His earlier building of 1668 can be seen to the right of the central building at right angles to it.

This was Christopher Wren's first completed building in Oxford and was designed in the French style. It was originally a free-standing building topped by a pediment and a high mansard roof. Unfortunately, the building was disfigured by "improvements" in 1802 which sacrificed the pediment and mansard roof. The original building can be clearly seen in David Loggan's famous birds-eye view of Trinity College contained in *Oxonia Illustrata* published in 1675.

A notable alumnus is Sir Harold Thompson, FRS, who was Chairman of the Football Association from 1976-1981. He founded Pegasus Football Club for blues of Oxford and Cambridge. Pegasus won the FA Amateur Cup in 1951 and 1953 at Wembley when this competition was one of the highlights of the national sporting calendar.

In those days the rewards for professional footballers were not great, so many players with good jobs did not turn professional.

The standard of amateur football was very high.

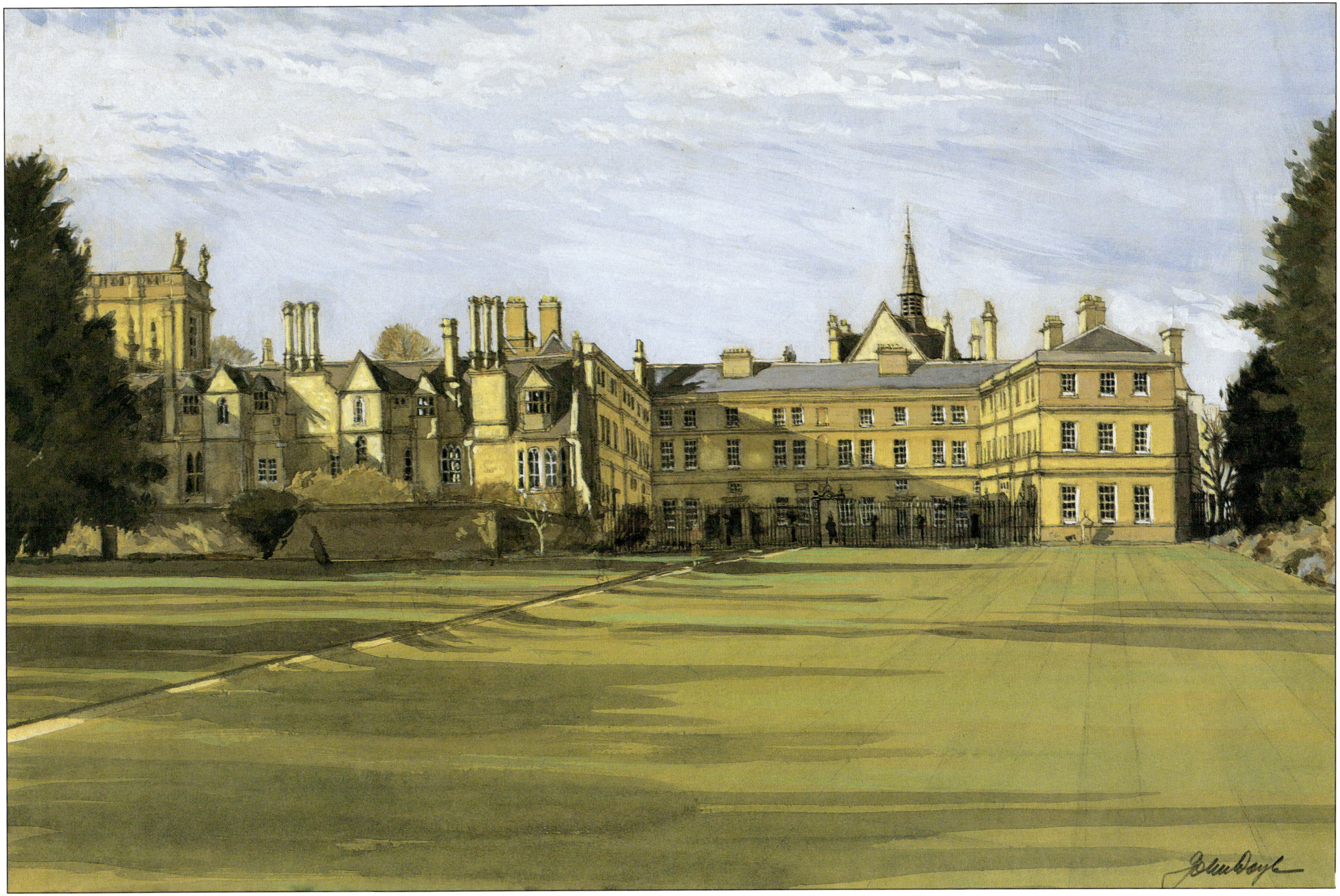
John Doyle

UNIVERSITY COLLEGE

Jane Carpanini

High Street Front

Univ, as University College is known, is generally accepted as Oxford's oldest college, being founded by William of Durham in 1249. Balliol and Merton have long disputed this claim.

As if to consolidate its claim, however, legend has it that Alfred the Great founded *Univ* in 872. Ralph Higden's *Polychronicon*, written in 1354, had claimed that Alfred, advised by St. Neot, had established "public schools for the various arts at Oxford". In the 1380s, during a lawsuit, the Fellows of University College went one better and claimed that Alfred had founded the College itself, a claim confirmed in 1727 by the Court of King's Bench in London. In more recent years, however, the College has accepted that Alfred's links with Oxford are merely legendary, and has been content to base its claim to seniority on William of Durham.

Between 1634 and 1677 the college completely rebuilt itself, including the addition of the first battlemented gate tower, shown in Jane Carpanini's painting, which contains the porter's lodge and has a stone statue of Queen Anne on the street front and one of her father, James II, on the inner front.

Also in Jane's painting can be seen the dome of the Shelley Memorial, under which resides a marble statue of the naked poet, Percy Bysshe Shelley, carved by Edward Onslow Ford in 1894. Shelley was an undergraduate of *Univ* but was expelled in 1811, after only two terms, for publishing *The Necessity of Atheism*. Sadly, he was drowned eleven years later.

Jane's watercolour is an unusual view of University College as seen from the High Street. Usually it is portrayed the other way round, looking towards Carfax, but the pronounced bend in The High loses *Univ's* perspective. Jane's view towards Magdalen captures the whole of the College front to great effect.

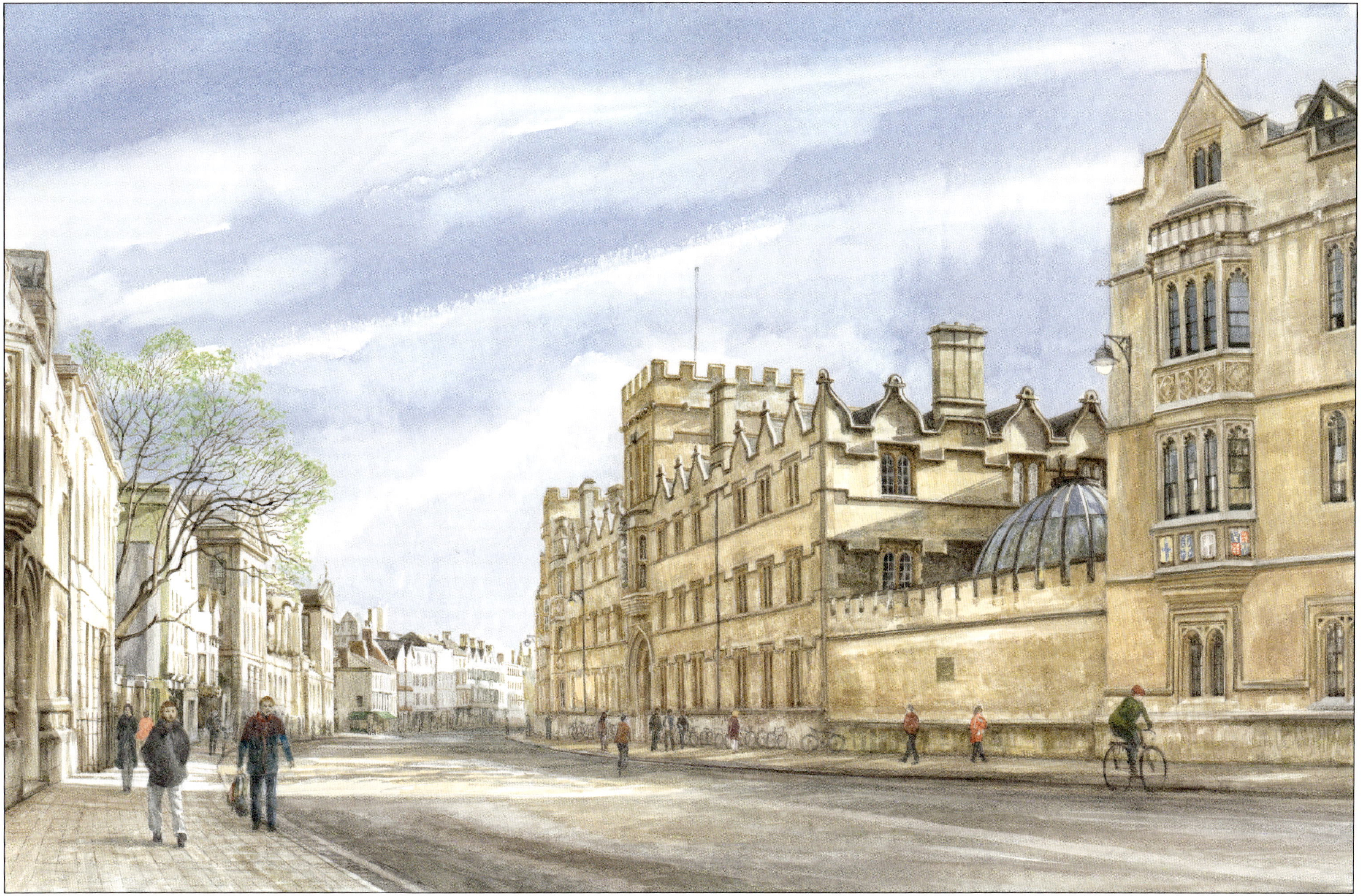

UNIVERSITY COLLEGE

Jane Carpanini

Radcliffe Quadrangle

One of *Univ's* most distinguished graduates was John Radcliffe, a wealthy and successful physician whose benefactions are everywhere to be seen in Oxford. The most important of these are the Radcliffe Camera, Observatory and Infirmary.

When he died in 1714, his estate also provided funds to build a quadrangle at University College on condition that it "be answerable to the old". It is thus a smaller version of the 1634 Front Quadrangle, and includes a castellated gate-tower containing a superb lead statue of John Radcliffe on the inner side, and another of Queen Mary II on the street front. *Univ*, therefore, is unique in having statues of the last three Stuart monarchs on its gate-towers – Queen Anne and King James II are on the others. Equally impressive is the fan vaulting below the tower. It is the last example in Britain of functional fan vaulting, as opposed to the merely decorative variety.

Jane Carpanini's pretty painting captures the aesthetic charm of this smaller quadrangle, which is more intimate than the larger Front Quadrangle on which it is based.

Univ can lay claim to two post-war Prime Ministers, Clement Attlee, a graduate, and Harold Wilson, a Fellow. Interestingly, the present Master, Lord Butler of Brockwell, served three recent Prime Ministers – Margaret Thatcher, John Major and Tony Blair – as Cabinet Secretary and Head of the Home Civil Service.

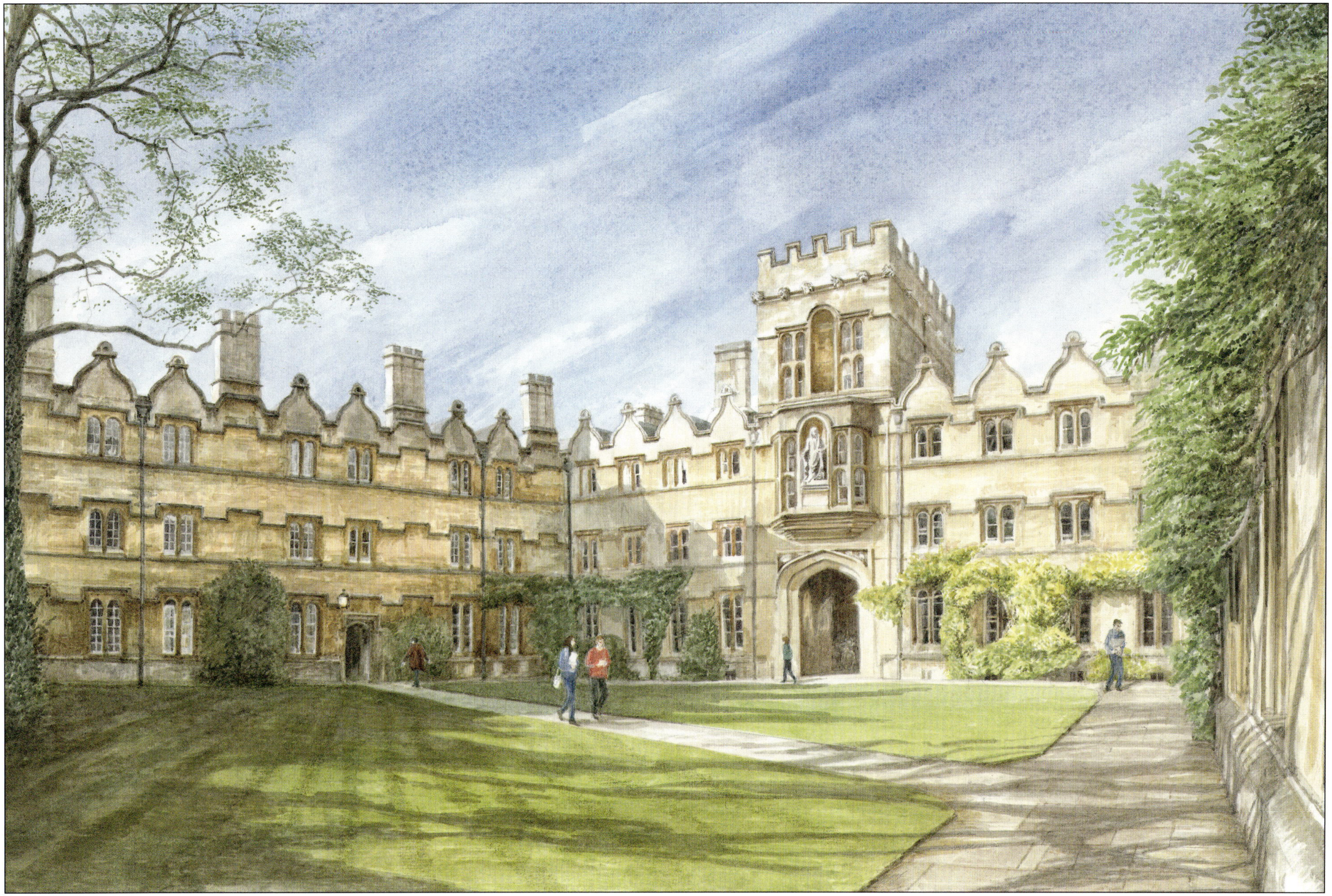

WADHAM COLLEGE

Dennis Flanders

Front Quadrangle

As you enter the Front Quadrangle from Parks Road through the fan-vaulted gateway, you are faced on the east range of the quad by three statues. They are of James 1, and Nicholas and Dorothy Wadham, and are situated centrally above the entrance to the impressive Hall, with its great hammer-beam roof.

Wadham was endowed in 1609 by a wealthy Devonian, Nicholas Wadham, on his deathbed. It was, however, his widow, who, after fighting off family designs on his estate, petitioned James I for a Charter.

She moved with great alacrity appointing an architect, William Arnold, well known to her for his work in the West Country.

She drew up the statutes and appointed the first Warden, Robert Wright, in 1613 – quite an achievement for a woman of 79 years. She directed operations from her home in the West Country, but never visited Oxford and so did not see her foundation.

In its early days, Wadham College was fashionable with the sons of west country gentry, including, in 1619, Carew Raleigh, son of Sir Walter, who had been executed the previous year.

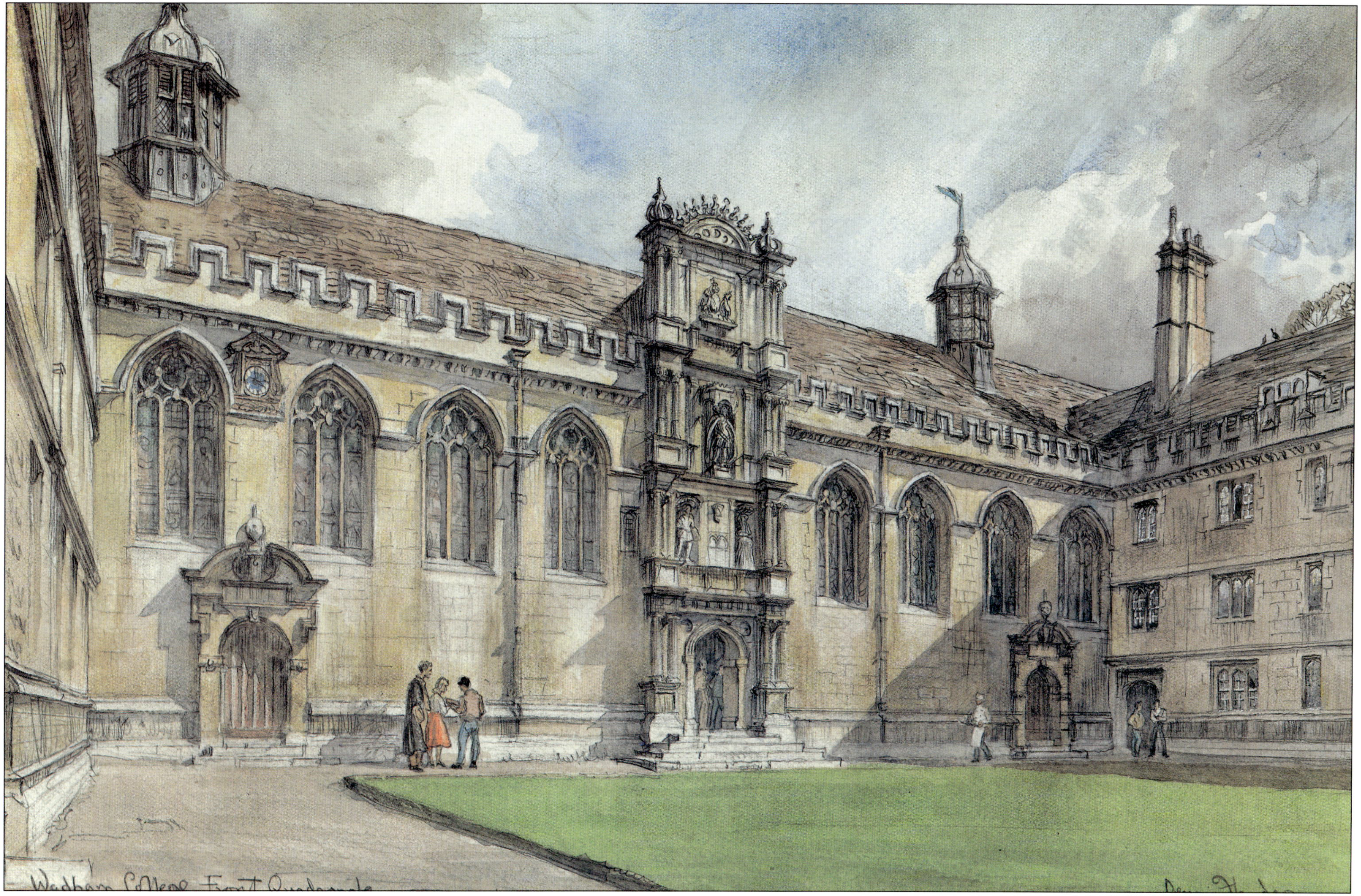
Wadham College Front Quadrangle

WADHAM COLLEGE

Dennis Flanders

Garden Front

In the summer of 1989, Dennis completed his painting of Wadham's Front Quadrangle and we took it back to the college to gain approval. A small sherry party was organized for that purpose by the late Dr Ralph Johnson, of the Development Office. The Warden, Sir Claus Moser, attended and views were expressed. Some people felt the subject was too austere and that a pastoral scene would be more appealing.

To reconcile the conflicting opinions, it was decided Dennis should produce a second painting of the renowned Garden Front from the Fellows Garden and the two should be produced as a contrasting pair.

Wadham's most illustrious Warden was perhaps Sir Maurice Bowra, who held that office from 1938 to 1970. He was a progressive and civilising influence well known for his hospitality – *I am more dined against than dining.*

The college expanded dramatically in numbers and academic reputation during his time as Warden and shortly after his term of office, Wadham was one of the first colleges to accept women.

A distinguished graduate of Wadham, in 1653, was Christopher Wren, whose most famous creation in Oxford is the Sheldonian Theatre. More recent alumni include Cecil Day Lewis, the Poet Laureate; Michael Foot, Deputy Prime Minister 1976-1979; and Melvyn Bragg, writer and television presenter.

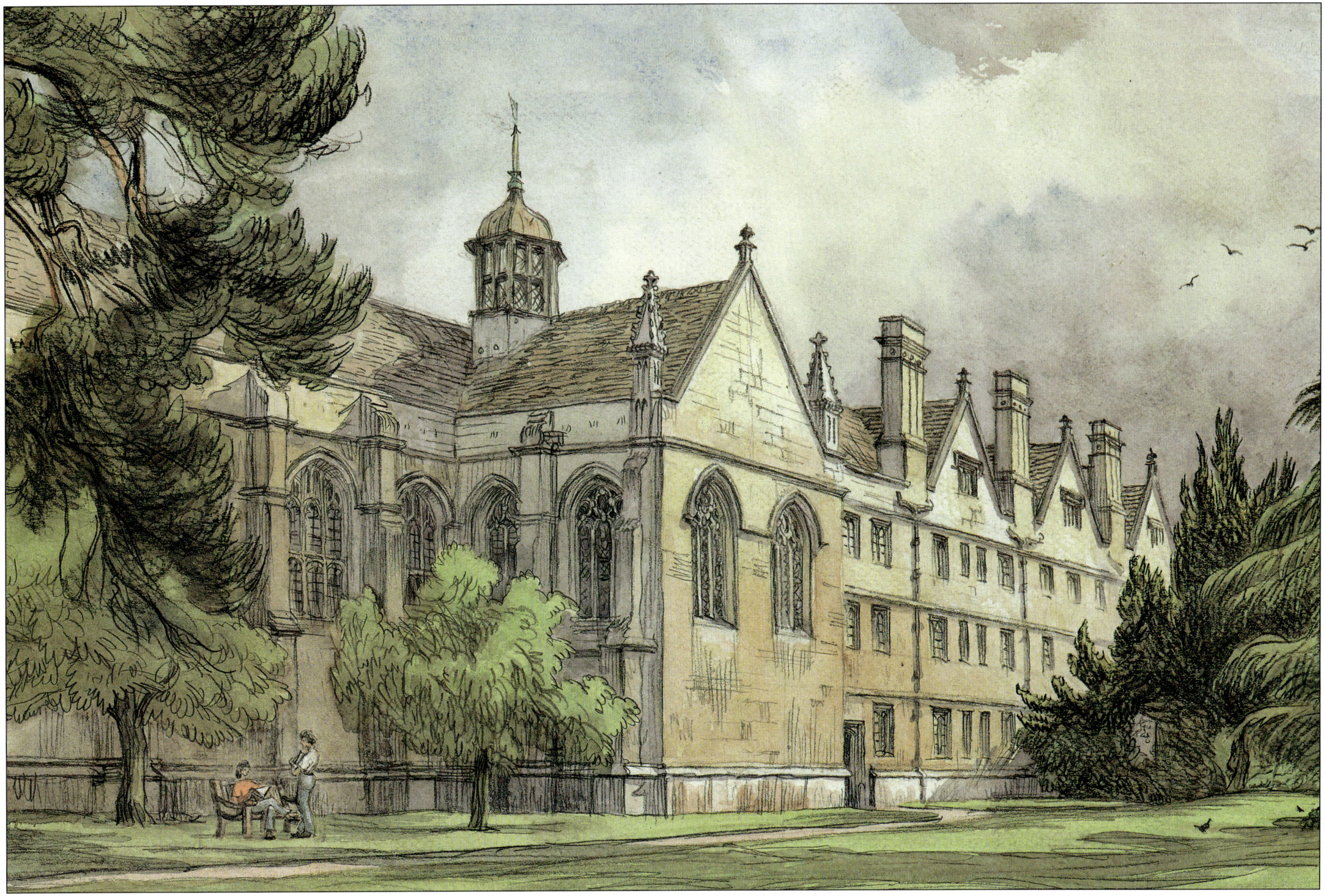

WORCESTER COLLEGE

Dennis Flanders

The College Quadrangle

In 1283, the Abbey of St Peter's Gloucester founded a small community on the site that is now Worcester College. In due course, other Benedictine monasteries were connected with Gloucester College and many built their own camerae. These origins are reflected in the cottages on the south side of the main quadrangle which display the arms of a number of abbeys.

When Henry VIII dissolved the monasteries in 1541, the site fell into his hands and was subsequently purchased in 1560 by Sir Thomas White, the founder of St John's College, which owned what then became Gloucester Hall.

In 1714, Gloucester Hall was refounded as Worcester College on a legacy from Sir Thomas Cookes, a baronet of Worcestershire, who bestowed his own arms and his county's name on the new foundation.

Rebuilding began to a plan attributed to Dr George Clarke, though he is known to have corresponded with Nicholas Hawksmoor about his design.

Almost all the cottages which ran along the north side of the quadrangle were demolished to make way for the elegant 18th century terrace building, but the money ran out, fortunately, before the cottages on the south side could be similarly replaced.

Beyond the lop-sided quadrangle are the gardens and lake which are part of that extra magic Alice saw in Wonderland when she looked through a gate into a beautiful garden (identified by some commentators as Worcester).

Dennis's drawing of the main quadrangle, viewed from the cloister under the 18th century library, is a poignant reminder of the college's chequered history.

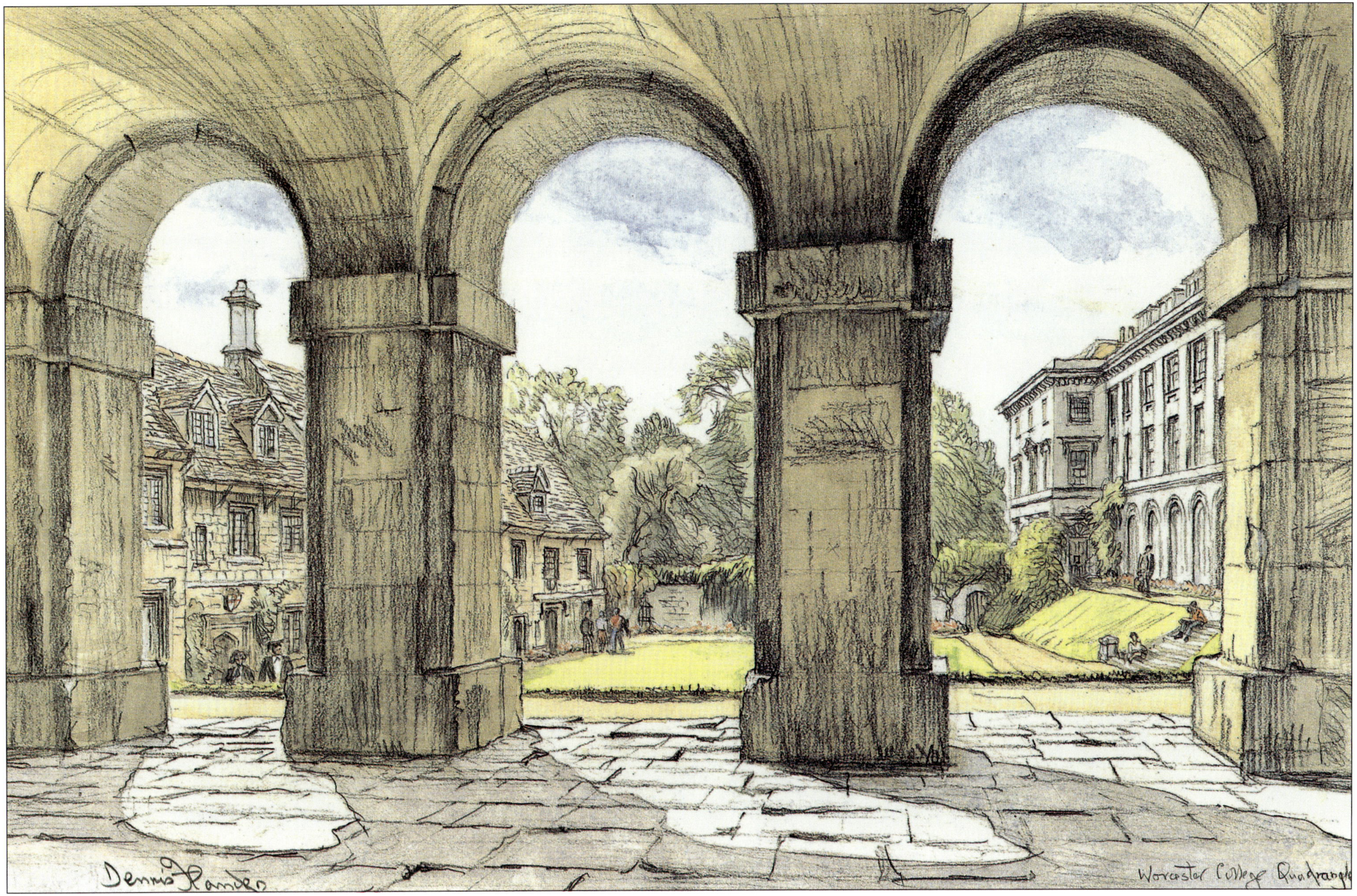
Dennis Flanders
Worcester College Quadrangle

WORCESTER COLLEGE

Dennis Flanders

The College Front

The approach to Worcester College was through fields and allotments until Beaumont Street was laid out in the early 19th century. The college persuaded the developer to put in the subtle curve which makes the whole effect so attractive. The entrance block was part of Dr George Clarke's design for the new college.

To the south, the projecting wings house the Hall, its interior now restored to the original design by James Wyatt, and to the north, the Chapel, which is decorated in exuberant mid-Victorian style by Burges. Between them runs the magnificent library. The front of the College is thus, functionally, its back, and the clock and the proximity to the railway station have prompted the remark: *'C'est magnifique, mais ce n'est pas la gare'.*

Dennis completed his painting of the College Front in August 1992, in the first year of Richard Smethurst's appointment as Provost.

As is usual when prints of original paintings are offered to past members, the Head of House writes a commendation urging members to purchase in order not only to acquire splendid mementoes of the college but also to help with college appeals.

I particularly liked Dick Smethurst's literary style and I can do no better than quote from the final paragraph of his commendation of both pictures of Worcester College: *"Undergraduates are setting off for Moderations, someone is incurring the Garden Master's wrath by standing on the lawn, and the tangle of bicycles along the front railings will soon be vigorously unravelled."*

What would Oxford be without lawns and bicycles?

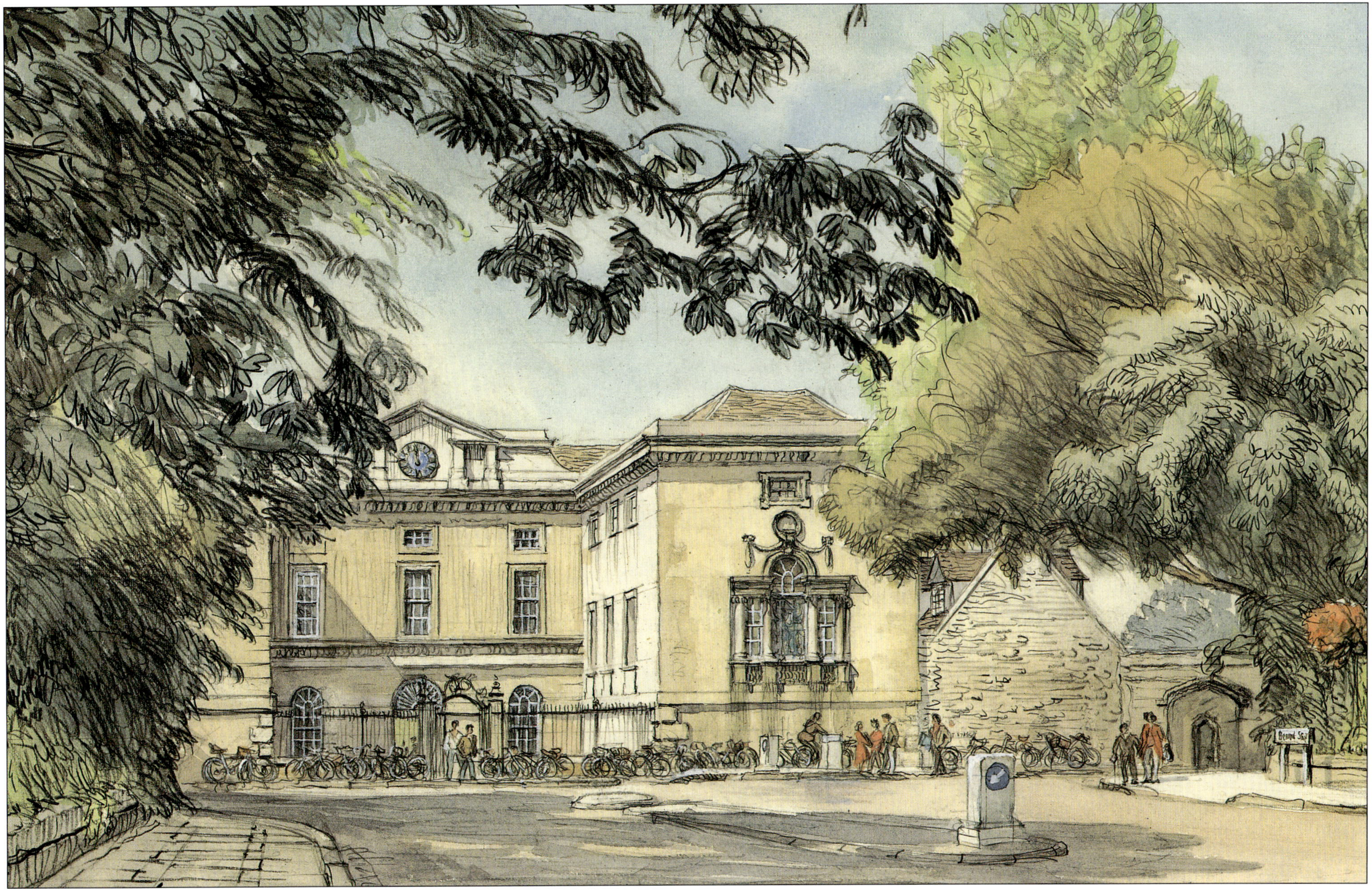

SEWANEE, USA – Exporting Oxford

Ken Howard

The Shapard Tower

An article under the heading *Exporting Oxford* appeared in the 1998 Hilary edition of the University magazine *Oxford Today*. It discussed attempts to replicate the unique elements of Oxford's collegiate system and architecture overseas.

One of the places mentioned was the University of the South, Sewanee, which is situated 2,500 feet above sea level on a plateau in central Tennessee. Its campus is an oasis of tranquillity set in 10,000 acres of the most beautiful woodland, with breathtaking views all around.

Founded by the leaders of the Episcopal Church in 1857, it has a student population limited to 1,400, with a teaching ratio of only 9:1. It has always had close links with the Church of England and Oxford University.

The integrity of its gothic architecture is amazing. One of its earliest structures, the Breslin Tower (1886), was modelled on Magdalen Tower Oxford, and all subsequent buildings have remained faithful to the gothic style, including the $12,000,000 Dining Hall which was recently completed.

As a result of the *Oxford Today* article I contacted Sewanee's Alumni Relations Director, Yogi Anderson, and suggested that they should, like Oxford's Colleges, participate in our watercolour print series.

Over a period of months arrangements were made, and Ken Howard was commissioned to produce three watercolours of Sewanee. He arrived at Sewanee via Chattanooga in November, 1999, spent a delightful week on the beautiful campus, and produced three evocative watercolours which Yogi described as "awesome".

The painting featured here is of the Shapard Tower which in 1959 completed the cathedral-like All Saints Chapel started in 1907. The tower was modelled on St Mary the Virgin, Oxford although the spire was changed to a lantern. Most of the chapel's stained glass, including a magnificent 20-foot diameter rose window, was executed by J Wippel and Co. Ltd of Exeter, in England, in 1958. The building to the right of the chapel is the eastern side of the Carnegie Hall, completed in 1913.

The University of the South maintains close links with Oxford, having summer schools each year in both Lincoln College and St John's College. Sewanee, however, is unique.

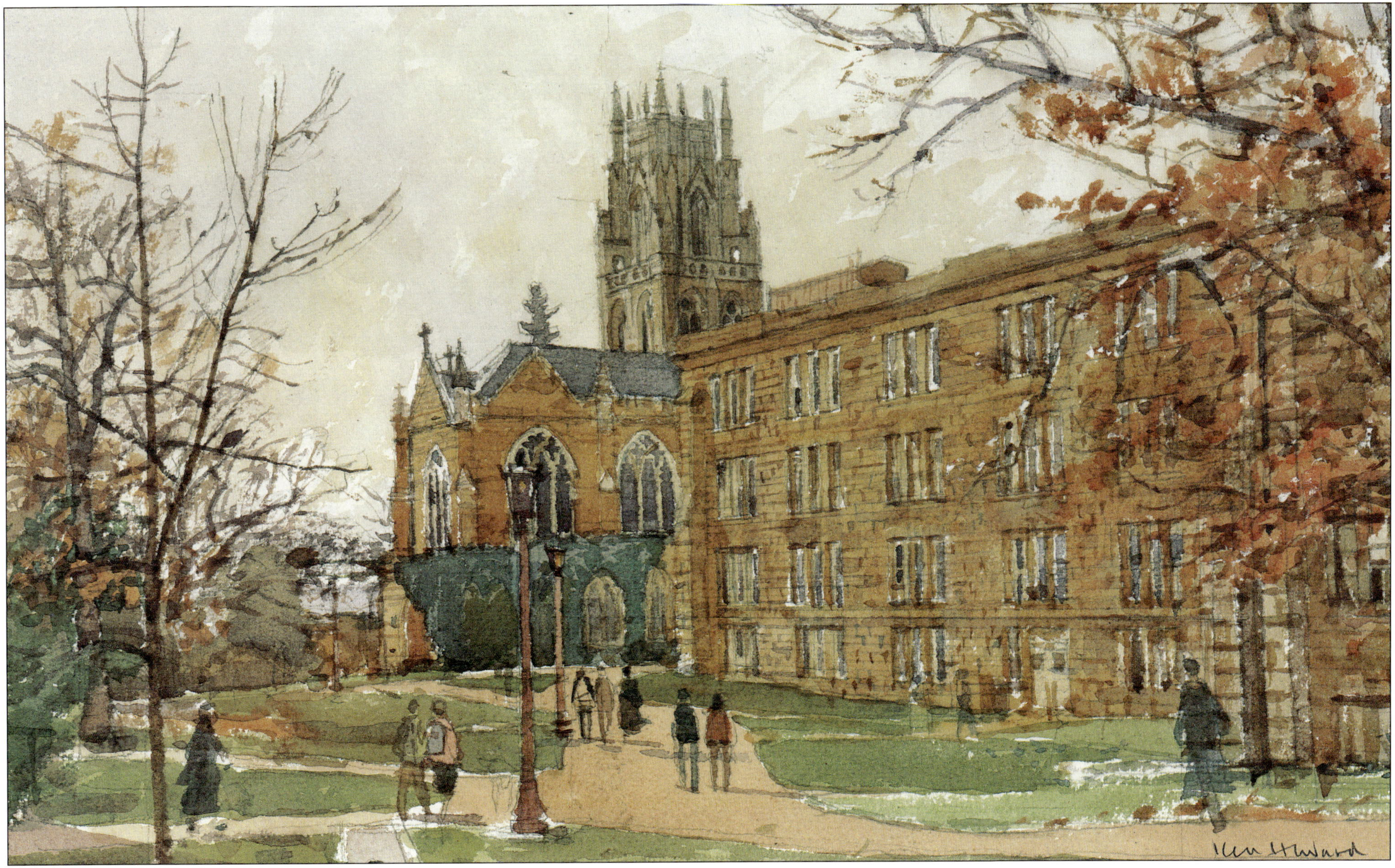
Ken Howard

MALCOLM HORTON, author and publisher

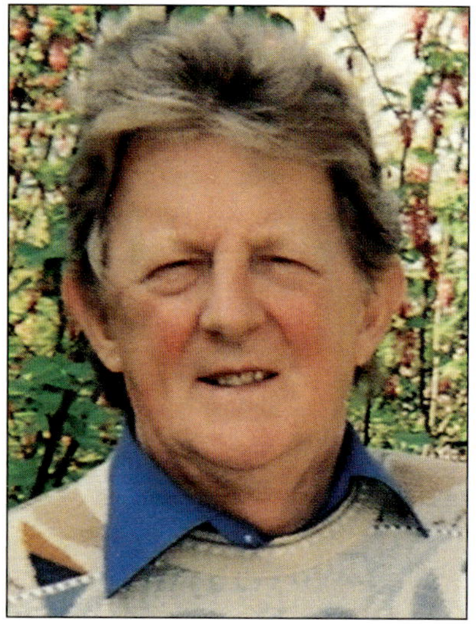

Malcolm Horton was articled to a City of London firm of chartered accountants and qualified in 1966. He spent twenty years in industry and commerce with companies such as Beck and Pollitzer, Esso Petroleum and BOC International. The latter part of this period was spent in the printing industry, where he was, successively, chief executive of Williams Lea, and of international fine art printers, Westerham Press. In 1986 he set up an accountancy practice as well as a fine-art publishing business, Contemporary Watercolours. The watercolour business has not only allowed him to work with some of Britain's most talented watercolour painters but his peregrinations have given him an intimate knowledge of the beautiful towns and cities of the British Isles, particularly Oxford. In his spare time Malcolm Horton was, in the 1970s, a borough councillor for the London Borough of Bexley, and in 1983 stood (unsuccessfully) for the SDP in the General Election. His one previous book, *Watercolours in Academe,* was published in 1995. His hobbies include playing squash and watching Charlton Athletic FC. He is married and lives with his wife Valerie on the Chart Hills, just outside Ashford in Kent.

INDEX OF COLLEGES